PRAISE FOR
FAITHFUL PRESENCE

"If you're burned out on political discourse in America, you're not hearing from voices like Bill Haslam. Refreshing, funny, nuanced, and insightful, this book will give you hope in the country you love."

—DONALD MILLER, AUTHOR AND CEO OF BUSINESS MADE SIMPLE

"In this era of perpetual outrage, one could easily conclude that the Sermon on the Mount cannot coexist with the *Federalist Papers*. Indeed, many seem to be giving up on either the idea of democracy itself or the hope that this democracy could produce—and demand—leaders of character and conviction.

This book shows a different way. I can think of no leader in public life who better exemplifies character, reasonableness, prudence, and tenacity more than Bill Haslam. This book takes the reader through major decision points in Governor Haslam's life while elaborating on how we could have a politics of principle and even humility. This book calls us away from the way of Machiavelli and toward the way of Jesus. This book is not just for those in or considering a political life, but for everyone who leads in any arena of life. This is the book we need right now, and it comes not a moment too soon."

—RUSSELL MOORE, PRESIDENT OF ETHICS AND
RELIGIOUS LIBERTY COMMISSION

"As our country seems to be more divided than ever, *Faithful Presence* seems to be written for such a time as this. Guided by his faith and leadership experience, and with refreshing humor and humility, Bill Haslam has written a book that takes on the complexities of being a Christian in public office. As a Democrat who served with Governor Haslam, I cannot recommend this book enough. Whether you are in elected office or not, it's a voice we need to help heal our nation."

—RAUMESH AKBARI, TENNESSEE STATE SENATE,
DEMOCRATIC CAUCUS CHAIR

"Bill Haslam has written a superb book on faith and politics, drawing on lessons from the Bible, history, and his own consequential life. *Faithful Presence* is engaging and insightful, challenging and candid, and oh-so-timely. In an age in which prominent figures have discredited the Christian witness in the political arena, Haslam shows us the way out and the way up. This book will give you hope."

—PETER WEHNER, *NEW YORK TIMES* OP-ED CONTRIBUTOR
AND SENIOR ADVISOR TO PRESIDENT GEORGE W. BUSH

"If you're concerned about the ways in which the Christian faith has become such a divisive factor in our national politics, *Faithful Presence* is the book you must read. At a time when our political discourse has devolved into a 'Hatfields vs. McCoys' kind of blood feud, Governor Bill Haslam offers a desperately needed third way—not angry divisiveness, not passive-aggressive conflict avoidance, but a way of humble and authentic engagement—with faith serving not as a political weapon but as a moral compass."

—RICHARD STEARNS, PRESIDENT EMERITUS OF WORLD VISION US AND
AUTHOR OF *THE HOLE IN OUR GOSPEL* AND *LEAD LIKE IT MATTERS TO GOD*

"Bill Haslam uses his remarkable political experience to explore how people who believe in truths beyond power politics can be a key part of healing the deep divides in our country. Perhaps people who understand the reality of the image of God in all of our neighbors—and who believe in the Gospels that free us to love unconditionally—can humbly point to a different way of living with even our scary differences."

—BEN SASSE, UNITED STATES SENATOR

"For too long, politics has been treated as an area of life in which Jesus is at a terrible disadvantage. Those who follow Jesus, then, are best advised to be involved in politics only to mitigate their losses, if even that. Of course, throughout American history—indeed, the history of politics around the world—there are countless examples of those who have acted in politics not to be served, but to serve.

Christians are called to be faithful in all of life, including politics, and the church desperately needs to hear and heed this call. My friend, Bill Haslam, is a Christian who has heeded that call. In *Faithful Presence*, you'll learn from someone who has been at the very height of our politics, who has borne the burden of political leadership, and insists faithfulness is the best way to meet the challenges of our day. I share Bill's conviction. I encourage people of every political persuasion to read this valuable book. Consider how your pursuit of faithfulness might influence how you think about political life and the positive contribution you can make."

—MICHAEL WEAR, AUTHOR OF *RECLAIMING HOPE: LESSONS LEARNED IN THE OBAMA WHITE HOUSE ABOUT THE FUTURE OF FAITH IN AMERICA*

FAITHFUL PRESENCE

FAITHFUL PRESENCE

THE PROMISE AND THE PERIL OF FAITH

IN THE PUBLIC SQUARE

BILL HASLAM

NELSON
BOOKS

An Imprint of Thomas Nelson

Published in Nashville, Tennessee, by Nelson Books, an imprint of Thomas Nelson. Nelson Books and Thomas Nelson are registered trademarks of HarperCollins Christian Publishing, Inc.

Published in association with the literary agency of Wolgemuth & Associates.

Thomas Nelson titles may be purchased in bulk for educational, business, fundraising, or sales promotional use. For information, please e-mail SpecialMarkets@ThomasNelson.com.

Unless otherwise noted, Scripture quotations marked ESV are taken from the ESV® Bible (The Holy Bible, English Standard Version®). Copyright © 2001 by Crossway, a publishing ministry of Good News Publishers. Used by permission. All rights reserved.

Scripture quotations taken from The Holy Bible, New International Version®, NIV®. Copyright © 1973, 1978, 1984, 2011 by Biblica, Inc.® Used by permission of Zondervan. All rights reserved worldwide. www.Zondervan.com. The "NIV" and "New International Version" are trademarks registered in the United States Patent and Trademark Office by Biblica, Inc.®

Any internet addresses, phone numbers, or company or product information printed in this book are offered as a resource and are not intended in any way to be or to imply an endorsement by Thomas Nelson, nor does Thomas Nelson vouch for the existence, content, or services of these sites, phone numbers, companies, or products beyond the life of this book.

ISBN 978-1-6836-6750-6 (audiobook)

Library of Congress Cataloging-in-Publication Data

Names: Haslam, Bill, 1958-author.
Title: Faithful presence: the promise and the peril of faith in the public square / Bill Haslam.
Description: Nashville, Tennessee: Nelson Books, 2021. | Includes bibliographical references. | Summary: "Two-term governor of Tennessee Bill Haslam reveals how faith—too often divisive and contentious—can be a redemptive and unifying presence in the public square"—Provided by publisher.
Identifiers: LCCN 2020038681 (print) | LCCN 2020038682 (ebook) | ISBN 9781400224425 (hardcover) | ISBN 9781400224432 (epub)
Subjects: LCSH: Christianity and politics—United States. | Christians—Political activity—United States. | Church and state—United States.
Classification: LCC BR516 .H325 2021 (print) | LCC BR516 (ebook) | DDC 261.70973—dc23
LC record available at https://lccn.loc.gov/2020038681
LC ebook record available at https://lccn.loc.gov/2020038682

Printed in the United States of America

21 22 23 24   LSC   10 9 8 7 6 5 4 3 2

For Crissy, the best First Lady in the history of forever, and an even better friend, wife, and mother. And to Will, Hannah, Annie, David, Leigh, and Matt, as hard as it is to be in politics, it is even harder to be in a politician's family. Thanks for loving me so well and for standing up for me even when I didn't always deserve it. I love all of you.

CONTENTS

—PROLOGUE—

The images are as jarring in hindsight as they were on that day. The US Capitol under siege by protesters. Windows smashed. A woman fatally shot. Demonstrators climbing on statues in the rotunda. Members of Congress huddled under their desks. A protester dangling from the balcony above the Senate floor across the inscription *Annuit Coeptis* (meaning "[God] has favored our undertakings").

On that same day, the country set a new record for deaths from the COVID-19 pandemic. This followed a summer of racial unrest, social justice protests, and a bitterly contested presidential election.

The entire country seems to be at each other's throats. Republicans are convinced that Democrats are socialists and them winning elections will mean the end of our country. Democrats are convinced that Republicans are racist with no concern for those the Bible calls "the least of these." Activists on the left and the right are convinced that only they represent "We the people" and vow to take back their government from the politicians.

The words of Isaiah ring true almost three thousand years later: "Justice is turned back, and righteousness stands far away; for truth has stumbled in the public squares, and uprightness cannot enter" (59:14).

How did we get here? And, more importantly, where do we go from here? If "truth has stumbled in the public squares," do we just give up on the public square as a place to solve problems?

Having served as a mayor and a governor, I know the

limitations of government and the wisdom of the psalmist's advice to "put not your trust in princes" (Psalm 146:3). But I also know that it matters who we elect, and it matters even more what they do and how they act after they are elected. Like we teach our children: decisions have consequences. Who we put in office and how we support those people make even more of a difference than I thought before I was in office.

Politics is the way that groups make decisions on how they will govern themselves so they can live together, whether it be your neighborhood association, a middle school student council, or a country. Like every other noble calling, politics can easily be twisted into a passionate pursuit of our own political success instead of a desire to serve. At its best, politics can be about wise, selfless decisions that mean better lives for people.

Unfortunately, it is far too common for politicians on both sides to play to the frustration and outrage of the voters they seek. Real leadership, however, is about connecting the legitimate problems facing those voters with the difficult reality of governing—and actually working to solve those problems.

While there is hope for solving a pandemic with a vaccine, there is no vaccine for the contemptuous polarization that grips us today. As the American experiment faces its greatest test since the Civil War, what can we, elected officials and concerned citizens, do to be faithful in such a time as this?

1

DIVIDED AND ANGRY

Some politicians write a book to set the stage to run for another office. Others write a book to be a memoir of their time in office. While those are valid reasons to write a book, and there are many good examples of those books, I am writing this book for a different reason.

I am writing this book because, like you, I am deeply concerned about the direction of our country. I am also writing because, though the idea might sound farfetched to some, I think people of faith can and should play a leading role in healing the wounds of this country. Unfortunately, that is not what has been happening. Too often the words and actions of Christians have done more to inflict those wounds than to heal them. But there is a better way.

It is no secret that we live in a divided nation.

The last nine presidential elections have been decided by single-digit margins—the longest streak in the country's history. No presidential winner has received over 55 percent of the vote since 1984, and the new president has received less than 52 percent of the vote in seven out of the last eight elections.[1] I do not see that changing anytime soon.

But we are not only divided; we are mad about it, and we cannot believe that the other side thinks the way they do. A January 2017 Reuters/Ipsos poll revealed that one in six Americans had stopped talking to a family member or a close friend because of the 2016 election.[2]

Of course, political division is nothing new in our country.

When Andrew Jackson was on his deathbed, he was asked if he had any regrets as he looked back on his life. Any who were expecting words of remorse, sympathy, or kindness would have been surprised by Jackson's purported reply. As the Congressional Record put it, "Old Hickory said he regretted he hadn't shot Henry Clay [the Speaker of the House] and hung John C. Calhoun [his own vice president]."[3] Things were similar for Alexander Hamilton, now best known as the subject of a hit Broadway musical. The politics of his day were so divisive that he was shot and killed in a duel by Aaron Burr, the sitting vice president. And this was only after Hamilton had narrowly avoided a duel with fellow founding father and future president James Madison.

But these times are different, and our divisions feel deeper. When Jackson's protégé James K. Polk was elected president, it took almost ten days for word of his electoral success to reach him at his home in Tennessee.[4] Today, the president's Twitter account can reach 100 million followers at the push of the Send button. Protests and counterprotests can be organized in the time it takes to compose an email or a text. A virtual protest can overwhelm a business or an individual before there is even time to organize a response. Every issue quickly takes on political undertones. A case in point is the COVID-19 pandemic. It did not take long before views on who was responsible for the outbreak and opinions on how to reopen the economy after the shutdown, and even whether or not to wear masks, took on strongly partisan tones.

Along with our division, and maybe at least partly due to that division, we see a growing concern about the direction of our society. The quality of our discourse continues to decline as people get used to hiding behind the anonymity and safety of the internet. As real community becomes a smaller part of our lives, many of us feel a growing sense of disconnection and decreasing hope for the future. We can see this played out in the rates of marriage and childbirth, two leading indicators of confidence in the future. The current marriage rate (6.5 unions for every 1,000 people) is the lowest since the federal government started keeping statistics right after the Civil War.[5] The fertility rate of 1.7 is also the lowest on record.[6] It takes a rate of 2.1 just to replace the population. And a larger percentage of births are happening outside of marriage. In 2016, estimates showed that about 40 percent of births in the United States occurred outside of marriage.[7] And on and on the list of items of cultural concern can go, with the only variable being who is making the list.

ENTER THE PEOPLE OF FAITH

In the midst of this division and concern about the country stand people of faith, who increasingly feel as if they have lost their bearings in this new world. Culturally, many feel as if they are on the outside looking in. Politically, success at the ballot box has not translated into the changes that many believers had hoped for and expected.

As the country grows more divided, our views on religion have only increased the disagreement. Christians are more and more confused about what role they should play in the public square or whether they should even care about the public square. And there is increasing resentment from people who feel that religion has too large a role in our public life. Americans are now more likely to say that churches and other houses of faith have too much influence in politics rather than too little.

The church has not been an exception to Americans' loss of

faith in institutions of all kinds. Confidence in the church has sunk to an all-time low. And, as the church continues to lose influence on mainstream culture, more and more people think that its loss of influence might be good for the country.

Nowadays, the term *evangelical* is more likely to be identified as a voting block than a description of someone who desires to share the good news of grace found in the Gospels. And it is not just people outside the church who are wondering about the church's role in politics. Among Christians, the debate about "a Christian view of politics" has grown only more contentious. The large block of evangelicals that supported the Trump presidency led to sometimes-heated conversations between Christians. In December 2019, when *Christianity Today* editorialized in favor of the impeachment of President Trump, battle lines were drawn within evangelical ranks.[8] This was the magazine founded by Billy Graham taking aim at political efforts led, in part, by his son Franklin Graham.

IS A FAITHFUL PRESENCE POSSIBLE?

The lines within the Christian community are as divisive as they are in the rest of the population. In a world where the political discussion has turned mean and contemptuous, and the political goal seems to be about keeping power rather than solving problems, Christians have frequently acted as mean and contemptuous as everyone else. Many Christians wonder if it is even possible to still have a faithful presence in the public debate. And those who still desire to be in the public square are left wondering what a faithful presence could look like in today's world.

I have served as a mayor and a governor. I have had a front-row seat and been a participant in politics and policy on local, state, and federal levels. My faith led me to make decisions that sometimes had my conservative friends upset with me and other times caused those on the left to rail against me—occasionally in the same week.

Within the idea of "one nation, indivisible" is the reality that our lives as Americans are marked more by disagreement and difference than unity. All of us, regardless of whether we claim to be people of faith, bring our own views about truth, goodness, and purpose to the public arena. We all bring our beliefs with us as we address public issues and decisions. The challenge in America has always been in how we live together respectfully when all of us describe the common good, and even the purpose of government, in different ways.

HOW DO YOU GET INVOLVED IN THE POLITICAL PROCESS—IN A FAITHFUL WAY?

Every man and woman has the right and responsibility to bring their most deeply held beliefs to the public square, where discourse, debate, and dialogue can flourish, as Lincoln said, "with malice toward none; with charity for all; with firmness in the right, as God gives us to see the right."[9]

How do we do that? Two leading Christian thinkers of our day, Tim Keller and John Inazu, expressed it this way:

> If our culture cannot form people who can speak with both conviction and empathy across deep differences, then it becomes even more important for the church to use its theological and

spiritual resources to produce such people. The Christian calling is to be shaped and reshaped into people whose every thought and action is characterized by faith, hope, and love— and to then speak and act in the world with humility, patience, and tolerance.[10]

The idea is that Christians, people who understand truth and compassion, should be able to show the world how to maintain kindness while expressing deepest differences, and thus help heal the deep divide in our country. I realize this is a preposterous idea to many people, Christians and non-Christians alike. But Christians have been called to be people of truth and love at the same time, even if we have often been guilty of having one without the other.

These times call for us to have a sound theology of political engagement so that our politics are driven by our faith, rather than our politics shaping our faith. All of us, whether we ever run for office or not, need a clear picture of what it means to be involved in the political process in a faithful way. But it rarely happens. My experience is that most Christians don't have a developed political theology, except for a position on a few issues like abortion, religious freedom, and gay marriage.

In other critical areas of life—marriage, raising children, student life, work life—Christians are exposed to count-less opportunities to develop their Christian view of that endeavor, such as books, videos, small-group studies, ser-mons, and more. The object of those teachings is usually on how to be salt and light—to act faithfully—in each of those particular areas rather than how to succeed in those areas at any cost. Student ministries focus on helping students live out their faith in today's challenging culture, not how to get a 4.0 on a report card. Discussions about a Christian view of business focus on our character and behavior in the marketplace, not how to get promoted or how to make your business a success.

Columnist David French wrote,

> Time and again in critical areas of life, Christians are rightly taught that the objective of the secular activity is less important than the manner with which you engage with your community. In every context commandments regarding our conduct aren't conditioned on levels of adversity. Duties of honesty and kindness don't slide away when bankruptcies loom or failures threaten our plans—even when those failures can have grave consequences for our lives.
>
> If you think, "Well, of course all this teaching should naturally translate to politics," then you're forgetting the inexorable pull of our fallen nature. . . . A voice whispers in our ears, saying, "You could be kind, but you'll lose. You could stand against lies, but you'll fail. All your worthy goals will turn to ash."
>
> And so—in the absence of the same kind of teaching that we receive in other vital areas of life—we're prone to conduct ourselves in politics differently than we do in virtually anywhere else.[11]

We slander our enemies on social media and pass along conspiracy theories as facts—behavior we would never see as acceptable in a nonpolitical context. Then we excuse ourselves by saying that the outcomes of our politics are so important that we are justified in our actions. This is what happens when we don't have a theology for our politics that helps our actions match our beliefs.

A CALL THAT'S CLEAR

This book is not just for people who are in public office or thinking about running for office. This book is for Christians who long to be salt and light in the public square—people who care deeply about this country and its future and who want their political actions to be a reflection of their faith. It is also for those who don't consider themselves Christians and have doubts about whether people of faith can contribute to the common good. Given our recent history, it's a legitimate concern. This book is for all of us who struggle to understand the right relationship between church and state, between our most deeply held beliefs and our role as citizens.

Christian or otherwise, red, blue, or purple, many of us are losing hope in a future that we once took for granted. There is a way for Christians to be at the center of restoring that lost hope. And it can happen in a way in which even nonbelievers will be glad to have us engaged in the public square.

As our country grows more polarized and people of faith become increasingly fearful about the growing secularization of the country, this is the right time to consider what it should look like for us to be engaged in the public square. It is my hope that Christians, in being faithful to the role God has called us to, will become people who help heal the political differences that are ripping our country apart. It is my hope that, rather than reacting out of fear of what we might be losing, we will engage as people who are committed to serving in the public square for the common good. While there will always be legitimate areas of disagreement among Christians in our political views, I am convinced that there are some things where our call is crystal clear.

Amid frustration over today's climate of partisan fights, not only is a faithful presence what Christians are called to have, but it can also be the answer to the hopelessness so many feel about our current political challenge. My hope is that this book will provide a vision for how Christians can become that answer. We will start with a look at our current political climate, the reasons behind our deep divisions and contempt for the other side, and the ways Christians have been shaped more by the partisan ideology of today's media and online life than by the formational practices of following Jesus.

We will then discuss whether or not a Christian response in today's world is realistic. Does having a faithful presence mean unilaterally disarming right when the stakes have never been higher in the public arena? Are humility and meekness nice ideas that don't really apply when we face opposition that is organized, formidable, and trying to push us out of the public square? Along the way, I will talk about what I learned from my time in the arena, from the difficulties of running for office to the challenges of trying to make decisions on pardons and clemencies that reflected justice and mercy.

Finally, we will look at what a faithful presence can look like today—and why I believe that Christians, as people of justice, mercy, and humility, can help the country move out of the angry spirit that grips it now. That will mean learning to stop being people who live out of our grievances about how the world hasn't treated us right and learning to react out of love rather than responding out of fear. In the process, we will look at how God can use our engagement in the public square to make us more like him, whether we are running for office or learning to be an informed voter and advocate.

REMINDING A WOUNDED AND WEARY NATION

I had been in office as governor of Tennessee about two weeks when Max Haston, the adjutant general of the Tennessee National Guard, asked me to attend the Guard's annual meeting on a Saturday morning. I arrived and was immediately taken to a holding room outside the main ballroom where the meeting was being held. Soon, a sergeant came to escort me to the back of the ballroom.

I was impressed by the sight before me. All the men and women of the Tennessee Air and Army National Guard were in the room in uniform. They were seated with their units, and at the end of each row were battle flags signifying all the nation's battles that unit had fought in over the years. I was at the back of the room looking down a long aisle to the podium. As soon as I arrived in position, a deep voice came over the speaker, saying, "Please welcome the commander in chief of the Tennessee National Guard." Immediately the entire group of soldiers and airmen rose to their feet and saluted as the band began playing. I was enjoying watching the pageantry of the event when the sergeant pulled on my arm and said, "Sir, that's you." That is when it dawned on me. I was the one who had just been announced. It was me that was being called to the front.

It is my hope that people of faith realize that we are the ones being called to bring hope to a world that feels increasingly divided. In these days of confusing situations, when the entire nation seems filled with contempt for the other side, perhaps we can model what Jeremiah was calling the Israelites to do in Babylon: "Seek the welfare of the city where I have sent you into exile" (Jeremiah 29:7). And, in doing that, we can remind a wounded and weary nation that there is One who came to rescue us from a life without hope.

2

WHAT IS HAPPENING NOW?

Every year the president of the United States, regardless of which party is in power, hosts a black-tie dinner for the governors of all the states and territories, and their spouses. The guests include the vice president and most of the cabinet. The US Marine Band provides music before everyone sits down to an elegant five-course dinner in the State Dining Room. Afterward, the guests are treated to entertainment in the East Room. Our first year in office, President Obama invited the band Earth, Wind and Fire to perform. I remember thinking what a uniquely American evening we were experiencing. Crissy and I were sitting with Nikki Haley, the first female Indian American governor in history, as our first African American president introduced the band to perform, with the larger-than-life portraits of George and Martha Washington flanking them in the East Room.

It was a night that Crissy and I always looked forward to attending. The highlight for us was usually the dinner conversations. Governors, cabinet secretaries, and members of the president's senior team were distributed throughout the room. With a mixture of Republicans and Democrats, the conversation was always polite, usually interesting, and occasionally fascinating.

One conversation stands out to me. It was February 2016, President Obama's last year in office. I was seated with one of the president's senior advisers. He described himself as a lifelong, passionate Democrat who had worked tirelessly to elect Obama in 2008 before joining the White House staff. I asked him what he knew now that he wished he had known eight years ago. "I wish I had known how hard this is. I wish I had known how difficult the issues are that come before the president. I would not have been so hard on George Bush. Don't get me wrong," he said, "I still do not agree with Bush's policies. But I have learned that this isn't easy, and the problems are a lot more complex and harder to solve than I thought."

I could not agree more. Most of the big problems we dealt with while I was in office were also a lot more difficult to solve than I anticipated. Whether it was lowering prison recidivism rates, improving the health of our citizens, or increasing literacy rates, moving the needle and showing measurable improvement was slower and more costly than expected, and the solution was less obvious than I wished. Whatever the issue, if it had made its way all the way to the governor's office, there was usually more than one idea worth considering as a solution. As my friend Herbert Slatery, the attorney general for Tennessee, says, "even a pancake has two sides." The best decisions were usually the result of fully considering both sides of an issue. Our best and most productive staff meetings usually involved a lively give-and-take, where every side of an issue was fully explored and debated.

Earlier I referred to the night at the White House as being "uniquely American." And by that I was not just talking about race. The reality is that every American is complex and different, and we all have our own perspectives. Leadership is accepting that reality as we try to solve our biggest problems.

MY RIGHT TO MY OUTRAGE

If my goal is to solve a problem and get to the best answer, I have found there are two keys: first, an awareness that my answer might not be the best answer; and second, a commitment to hear the other side of the argument. The conference room in the Tennessee governor's office had twelve seats around a large table. After my first year, I intentionally moved my seat from the head of that long table to the middle so I could be a part of the discussion instead of the one directing the outcome. More often than not, our final answer was a better solution than where we started.

Unfortunately, today's political climate is not very conducive to hearing the other side of any argument. To begin with, it is not as lucrative for those in the news business to explain the merits of both sides. The growth of social media and the cable news networks has also meant the growth of what Arthur Brooks called the "outrage industrial complex."[1] In the 1950s, Dwight Eisenhower talked about the growth of the "military industrial complex," those entities that benefit from the growth of the military and have an economic incentive to keep that going. As a former five-star general, Eisenhower had credibility when he talked about the growth of all the companies that profited from our defense budget.

Today, many news entities have an economic incentive to outrage. Stoking the fires of disagreement can be very profitable. Networks like CNN, Fox, and MSNBC have all learned that there is money to be made from emphasizing only one side of an argument. The madder I get at one side, the more I watch whoever is telling me how horrible that side is. Print and electronic news sources have learned that inflammatory articles get read or clicked on a lot more frequently than informative articles. Given that reality, what are we to do in this environment? How do we get an accurate picture of what's going on?

Forty years ago, we all pretty much got our news from the same places. Most people counted on their local newspaper and one of the three major television networks to tell them what was happening around town and around the world. Today, our choices are almost unlimited. Most Americans have more than five hundred programming choices on their televisions. Those cable channels provide around-the-clock access to news from whatever perspective you prefer, usually preceded by a header running across the screen screaming BREAKING NEWS any time of the day. Not only can we now get the news from a wide variety of sources, we can choose to hear the news all day long from whichever side we want.

Executives from Fox and MSNBC have told me that one of the things that surprises them most about their viewers is the number of people who leave the channel on all day, continuously streaming the news. Although those viewers are frequently just hearing the same news repeated in the loop, they want to make sure they don't miss anything. I understand.

Growing up, the first thing I did after waking up was head out to the mailbox to get the newspaper. While most kids were searching for Saturday morning cartoons, I was always reading the morning newspaper. I would even go get the newspaper early when I was spending the night at a friend's house. I never understood how they could just leave the newspaper out there in their driveway all morning long!

For my parents, the morning paper was their first chance to read about whatever happened the day before. For me, it was my first chance to read the sports section before my dad or older brother claimed it through breakfast. Today, most of us catch up with the news by scrolling through our phone before we get out of bed, even though we might have checked it right before we turned out the lights the night before.

This means that at any time of day, with a flick of a finger, we can easily choose a news source that tells us what we already think to be true. Confirmation bias is a real thing. We all want to hear information that confirms what we already believe. We like consuming news that tells us we are right. If we hear something that goes against what we believe, we either ignore it or declare it fake. And, if it is ambiguous, we tend to interpret it as supporting our existing position.

If that is not enough of a filter, then our phones will help us filter the news even more to our liking. The more we click on a certain topic or news source, the more our news feed service will prioritize similar items to our feed. So, not only do we choose our news, but then our news chooses us so we will keep viewing more of it.

THE PROFIT MOTIVE FOR SENDING OUT THE NEWS

It is important to remember that the media companies are businesses with profit motives. I do not say this as a criticism. I believe capitalism, though it has its shortcomings, is the best economic system. But we must remember that every media business has a need to attract an audience. Thus, the more "must-see" news they carry, the better the business results for the company.

During the 2016 campaign and the rise of Donald Trump from improbable candidate to president of the United States, Les Moonves, then the CEO of CBS, said regarding the Trump candidacy, "It may not be good for America, but it's damn good for CBS." He went on, "Man, who would have expected the ride we're all having right now? . . . The money's rolling in and this is fun. . . . I've never seen anything like this, and this is going to be a very good year for us. Sorry. It's a terrible thing to say. But, bring it on, Donald. Keep going."[2] Even CNN, the network that would spend the next four years complaining about Trump as president, went to great lengths to highlight Trump during the Republican primary debates in 2016. The minute the debate was over, they would invite then candidate Trump to be the first person to have an on-camera interview and give his view of the debate their viewers had just watched.

You cannot pay for that kind of advertising.

If you go into any newsroom today, you will see a digital scorecard on the wall measuring the number of clicks each online article has received. If a topic draws a lot of interest, there is sure to be multiple follow-up articles. This is the new business model keeping many companies afloat.

For many media companies, the best business model has turned out to be outrage. The most popular cable news shows, whether it is a smug Sean Hannity on the right or a smirking Rachel Maddow on the left, are premised on viewers sharing the host's outrage enough to make their viewing a habit.

THE SHORTEST INTERVIEW OF ALL TIME

During my second year in the governor's office, we passed a bill that changed the way state employees were hired and promoted. The state of Tennessee, like most governments, has a system of civil service rules in place to govern the hiring of employees as well as promotions and potential dismissals. The system gave preference to length of service, rather than performance, in all hiring and promotion decisions. The original intent of civil service laws was to prevent the governor (or mayor or president) from hiring only his or her cronies and firing everyone who worked for the previous administration.

Like a lot of good ideas with good original intentions, this one had developed some negative side effects. The decision of who was hired or promoted now depended primarily on who had been in line the longest. I don't know about you, but I have never felt like breathing in place should be the primary criteria for choosing someone to provide critical services to our citizens. There is great value in long service, but it is not the only factor in selecting and promoting the best people; our most important measurement must be quality of service to our citizens. After three months of a very involved legislative process, and an even longer time of trying to get everyone's input on the bill, we passed the TEAM Act. I think it is one of the most impactful things we did in office.

That afternoon, our communications director came into my office to say that Fox News wanted me to come on the air to talk about the bill. I agreed, and it was scheduled for later that day. Typically, for interviews on a national news show, I sit in a studio with a fake background of the Nashville skyline behind me. While I can hear the host in my earpiece, I am staring into a camera and cannot actually see the host in New York.

The show's host immediately began by asking what kind of fight there had been to get the bill passed. After I explained the process, he asked, "What about the employees' union? Didn't they fight you? I am sure there must've been lots of protests and shouting." I replied that we had worked with the employee groups and made some accommodations and that, while there were certainly things they didn't like about the bill, the head of the Tennessee State Employees Association had stood next to me when I signed the bill earlier that day. He asked again, "So there wasn't a big shouting match with threats of a government shutdown?" I told him no. I explained again that we had worked hard on the front end to listen to the objections, so we were able to pass a bill that met our purposes without a big fight. My answer was followed by the rarest thing on television today: a period of silence. Having quickly surmised that there was no exciting fight to recount here, the interviewer thanked me and ended one of the quickest interviews of all time. If there weren't going to be any fireworks, it was time to move on.

Liberal or conservative, we all appreciate news more when someone confirms what we already think. This leads to all the unfortunate side effects that we see in our divided world today. When we hear only one side of an argument, the one we were predisposed to agree with, we never appreciate the complexity of the issue. We become more convinced than ever that our answer is the right answer, and angrier than ever that the other side cannot see the truth. It becomes a vicious cycle as we give in to *confirmation bias* and choose to watch or read only the news that caters to our one side of the argument.

Like politicians who double down on appealing to their base rather than trying to persuade new voters, news outlets appeal to their market by focusing on what their viewers want to hear, which often includes, not surprisingly, fireworks. The next time you see a big news event, flip from cable channel to cable channel and note the difference in coverage.

The now infamous tape of Donald Trump and Billy Bush talking on an *Access Hollywood* show is a case in point. I had been on the road all day moving between events when the story broke. While I kept hearing about the remarks, I didn't see the tape until I got back to the Governor's Residence late that evening. When I turned on the TV, the difference in coverage was startling. I cannot imagine that CNN would have covered Pearl Harbor with any more sense that the world had changed forever. Meanwhile, Fox was covering a hurricane somewhere off the East Coast that had a very small chance of making landfall.

If you don't believe you are subject to confirmation bias, pay attention to how you read or watch the news. Look for how much time you spend reading articles that agree with your own view compared to the time you spend on items that do not match your point of view. Or notice how fast you change the channel when you do not like what you are hearing. Repeated studies have shown that we all tend to linger over news that we like and rush past those things that do not conform to our view.[3] If you do not believe climate change is a real problem, articles that seem to disprove that the earth is warming up will draw your attention. If you are in favor of more restrictive gun laws, you will tend toward articles that equate violent crime rates with the percentage of people who own firearms.

The truth is, most of us read the news to gain ammunition, not information. I know it always took me much longer to read the news on those rare days when the media had something nice to say about me. Conversely, when I saw a negative headline, it was a pretty quick read.

When you combine our bias toward news that confirms what we already believe, our ability to select our own news sources, and the media's economic need to continuously attract eyeballs, the end result is the passionately polarized political world of today. Is it really a surprise that the most watched cable news shows feature one person speaking or yelling while another person is talking over them? Sometimes I think there should be a rule that every show that includes a panel of experts should also include a first-grade teacher who reprimands anyone who speaks when someone else is talking! Television producers have learned that passion sells much better than nuance, even when nuance is almost always involved in the complex decisions that face our leaders. And we the audience encourage them to do that with our desire for simple answers to complex problems.

WE ARE DIVIDED—AND MAD ABOUT IT

So where does that leave us? We are divided. We are mad. And we cannot believe that the people on the other side cannot see it our way. We assume the other side must not be paying attention, or they must have bad motives. And our desire to attribute bad motives to the other side only adds to the combustible mixture.

A 2014 article in *Proceedings of the National Academies of Sciences* discussed what they called "motive attribution asymmetry." That is a mouthful of a term to describe what happens when you believe that your ideology is based on love and your opponent's motivation is based on hate.

The study revealed that a majority of Democrats and Republicans today have a level of motive attribution asymmetry that is equal to that of Palestinians and Israelis. Their conclusion was that Republicans and Democrats, like Israelis and Palestinians, are so suspicious of each other's motives that they find it impossible to ever find a compromise solution.[4]

That was back in 2014, and I think it is reasonable to assume that the feelings between Republicans and Democrats have only gotten worse since then. The phrase "harder to solve than peace in the Middle East" has long been used to describe a situation that appears impossible to solve. Now it looks as if we cannot approach some of our biggest disagreements, from soaring debt to climate change, with an attitude and expectation of a resolution.

Historically, many of our best policy outcomes have been the result of Democrats and Republicans coming together to solve a problem. Neither side got exactly what they wanted, but we addressed an issue that needed to be worked out for the country to move forward. Today, because both sides think the other side is not only wrong but wrongly motivated, it is rare to see anyone work across the aisle to come up with a solution. *Compromise* now means "lack of conviction," and it has become a dirty word. When you consider that the country is split almost evenly on political issues, and the partisans on both sides doubt the motives of the other side, it is easy to see why we often end up in a stalemate. It becomes a standoff, and neither side wants to budge.

IS THIS ANY WAY TO SOLVE PROBLEMS?

As my time as governor neared the end, Senator Lamar Alexander announced that he would not run for reelection when his term ended in 2020. The timing was perfect for me to run for the Senate. I could take a year to rest and get organized in 2019 and then prepare for a campaign in 2020. I had loved my fifteen years in office, beginning as mayor of Knoxville in 2003, and I liked the thought of taking a short break before hopefully resuming a role in public service.

Crissy and I spent several months thinking and praying about running. It was by far the most difficult vocational decision I have had to face. There are only one hundred Senate seats, and an open seat is a rare political opportunity. In the end, we decided not to run for a lot of reasons. For one, while most people think all political roles are the same, in reality, a legislative job like senator is very different from the work of a governor. The more I thought about it, the more I realized that the things I liked about being a mayor and a governor had very little to do with the role of a senator.

Perhaps the biggest thing that discouraged me from running, though, was a sense that players on both sides of the Senate were unwilling to tackle the tough issues facing the country. While deciding whether to run, I talked to a lot of senators. Almost all of them liked serving, but most had a story about attempting to do something to address one of our big problems and getting nowhere. Many of them had concluded that only incremental change was possible and that they would no longer even attempt to try to solve the big problems. The nature of our politics has grown so passionately partisan that no one is willing to stick out their neck to attempt important but difficult solutions. Most conclude that doing the hard stuff is just not worth it; it subjects you to either the fiery animosity of a social media blitz from those who like the status quo or the vitriol from those who would rather not solve any problem if it means giving an inch of ground to the other side.

Just twenty-five years ago, only 25 percent of Republicans and Democrats had a very unfavorable view of the other side. Today, the number of people with a very unfavorable opinion of the other side has soared to 55 percent.[5]

We are not just divided by parties; we are even divided by where we live. America is increasingly split between those who live in cities and those who don't. David Wasserman of the *Cook Political Report* has done a fascinating study about the different voting trends in counties with a Whole Foods store versus counties with a Cracker Barrel restaurant. Whole Foods tend to pop up in areas that can be described as urban and progressive, while Cracker Barrel often caters to a suburban or rural market.

In 1992, when Bill Clinton defeated George H. W. Bush, what some have called the "organic versus nostalgia gap" was around 19 percent. This gap had grown to 30 percent by the time George W. Bush ran against Al Gore in 2000. Eight years later, Barack Obama defeated John McCain with an aid of an over 40 percent gap. And in 2016, the gap soared to over 50 percent in the contest between Donald Trump and Hillary Clinton.[6]

Why does this matter? Since we all tend to live near, worship alongside, and associate with people who think like we do, it becomes even more difficult to understand the other side. If it seems like everyone we know thinks like we do, it's all the easier to assume the other side must be wrong.

So at a time when problems are more complex than ever, it has become increasingly difficult to solve problems. While listening to the other side of the argument has always been an important part of leading, our current environment is much more conducive to being outraged at the other side and assuming they are not only wrong but wrongly motivated.

Amid the division, Americans have drifted into one of two ways of approaching political involvement. The first group is passionate about their opinions, dug in, and frustrated at the other side. The second group is just exhausted and fed up with both sides.

We are divided, and we increasingly not only don't agree but doubt the motives of the people on the other side. Solving our big challenges has become more difficult than ever. At this point, the reader might reasonably ask, what does all this have to do with faith in the public square? And where are people of faith in this rapidly changing world?

Let's dig into that further next.

3

CONFUSED, INEFFECTIVE, AND EXHAUSTED

Jesus' message in the Sermon on the Mount was very clear: be different. The salt was supposed to be different than the meat. The light was supposed to be different than the dark (Matthew 5:13–16). In case we missed it, Paul reinforced the message when he told the church at Rome, "Do not be conformed to this world, but be transformed by the renewal of your mind" (Romans 12:2).

As the world becomes angrier and more divided, our path in the political arena is not always clear. But it is clear what we are not supposed to be: like the rest of the world.

Something has gone terribly wrong. When it comes to our engagement in the public square, Christians are not very different from everyone else. We, too, have become immersed in outrage stories. We, too, have become outspoken advocates without taking time to understand the arguments of the other side. We, too, are always ready to doubt the motives of our opponents and speak with contempt about their policies—and just as likely to take a shot at the other side on Facebook or Twitter. Too often, Christians are empowering these trends rather than resisting them.

And, most critically, we seem to be more worried about losing our country than we are about losing our God. Too many of us see the public square as a place where we can use God for our own desires and ends rather than be used by God for his desires and ends. Too many of us have sold our birthright as citizens of the city of God, choosing instead to bear up our swords to battle for our piece of the city of man. What is needed in America today is a group of people who are different, who are walking in their birthright as citizens of the city of God—a movement powerful enough to push the country in a new direction.

I cannot count the number of times I have seen wonderful examples of people of faith using their talents and treasure to bring about a better society. When I was mayor of Knoxville, Hurricane Katrina hit the Gulf Coast. As it became apparent that more and more residents of Louisiana would need to be evacuated, the Federal Emergency Management Agency (FEMA) put out a request for cities to host evacuees. Almost immediately the churches in our city—urban, suburban, and rural—volunteered their people and buildings to welcome those who had lost their homes. As governor, no matter where I went in the state, it always seemed that it was the church that was taking the lead on issues ranging from unequal education opportunities to health care in underserved areas.

Unfortunately, I have also seen how easy it is to hurt our cause by our political actions. When our politics direct our faith, rather than our faith directing our politics, we end up in the wrong place. Too many of us react out of fear and anger when it seems that the country is not going in the direction we want it to go.

During the Katrina crisis, we developed a protocol for receiving the people FEMA sent our way. We wanted to make sure that, in the midst of the horrible circumstances, the evacuees felt as welcome and comfortable as possible while they were with us. FEMA was using a combination of National Guard aircraft and chartered commercial aircraft to fly people out of New Orleans. We placed teams of people at our airport to greet them and provided transportation to where they would be staying. The colonel of our Air National Guard facility and I boarded each plane to welcome them to Knoxville and explain the logistics of their next move.

The initial flights were well organized and went off without a hitch. Meanwhile, back in New Orleans, circumstances were deteriorating. As time went on, voluntary evacuations turned into mandatory evacuations. By the time our last couple of planes arrived, most of those passengers had been forcibly evacuated from their homes or from the streets of New Orleans. It became apparent that the primary objective of FEMA was to make certain that these folks got out of New Orleans before conditions worsened.

When our final planeload of evacuees arrived, the situation onboard was nearly indescribable. (I'm told one of the evacuees on the flight later wrote a book about his experience and described me as "some dude in a tie, smiling like a game show host.") The plane was a chartered Delta aircraft. When I boarded, I saw the flight attendants huddled together in the galley. Even the air marshal on the flight seemed afraid. The cabin was full of an interesting slice of New Orleans nightlife. After all, these folks were the last to leave, and they left only because they were forced. There were numerous dogs roaming around the cabin. One woman had a snake wrapped around her neck. More than a few had terrified looks on their faces.

When I boarded the plane and said, "Welcome to Knoxville, Tennessee," the cabin erupted in shouting. It seemed that, in their urgency to get everyone out of New Orleans, the authorities had been telling people whatever they needed to tell them to get them on the plane. Almost all the passengers were told they were going somewhere besides Knoxville. Most were mad, confused, or afraid. I kept hearing, "This is not where I wanted to go."

Too often, Christians have reacted like the people on that flight. We thought our society was going to end up somewhere else. As our culture seems to grow increasingly secular, we have landed in a place we did not want to go. The days of daily Bible verses being printed in the newspaper and the Ten Commandments being posted in the classroom are mostly gone. Church attendance is no longer a cultural expectation, and Sundays are for Starbucks, not Sabbath worship. The fastest-growing religious affiliation for Americans is "none," with 26 percent of the population now describing themselves as atheist, agnostic, or "nothing in particular."[1] The definition of marriage has changed, even as marriage and beginning a family are being pushed off until later in life. As one friend noted, "Culturally, it feels like we went from being the home team to the visiting team in my lifetime."

The apostle Peter was no stranger to reacting out of fear in a world that seemed to be slipping away. On the night before he died, Jesus walked in the Garden of Gethsemane with his disciples. Tipped off by Judas, soldiers approached Jesus to arrest him. Peter, fearful that this could mean the end of his vision for Jesus to gain political power, pulled out his sword and took a swing at one of the men. Before Jesus could tell Peter to put away his sword, Peter had cut off the ear of a servant of the high priest.

This younger Peter seems a far cry from the older and wiser Peter who instructed us, "Always [be] prepared to make a defense to anyone who asks you for a reason for the hope that is in you; yet do it with gentleness and respect" (1 Peter 3:15).

For most of us, that is the problem. We don't know how to do that. We don't know how to give a defense for the hope that is in us, and we certainly don't know how to do it with gentleness and respect in a world that is rapidly changing. We have not thought through what we believe and why we believe it; we have only built a fear of what the other side might do and what we might lose. Fear is always a bad beginning place. As Nietzsche said, "He who fights with monsters should be careful lest he thereby become a monster."[2]

Not only have we not taken time to understand the other side's arguments, we have no understanding of our own blinders and misconceptions. Driven by the passions of today's political debate and inflamed by media focused on cultivating outrage, our language and actions look just like everyone else's. The polarization of politics has tempted all of us to pick sides in this increasingly bitter battle. What has been lost is the people of faith asking ourselves the hard questions about whether or not our politics match what we say we believe. Do our political actions match our theology, or has our theology been taken captive to our political beliefs?

WHOSE SIDE ARE WE ON?

During the Civil War, Abraham Lincoln once famously said, "My concern is not whether God is on our side; my greatest concern is to be on God's side, for God is always right." It was Machiavelli, not Jesus, who argued that the ends justify whatever methods we use to accomplish them. But today, many Christians seem to have concluded that Machiavelli was right and Jesus had it wrong. They have determined that we have to choose between being faithful and being politically effective. According to Machiavelli, one could not be a good Christian and a good citizen of the republic because being a Christian meant acting out of humility, grace, sacrifice, and forgiveness, whereas being an effective citizen meant "above all, assertion of one's proper claims in the knowledge and power needed to secure their satisfaction."[3] In other words, making sure we get the results we want is good citizenship.

In this way of thinking, a candidate who will support our view on abortion, or the expansion of health-care coverage, or any other issue that we deem worthy, is to be supported at all costs. So, the ends of having power is worth abandoning our biblical principles in order to elect the right people and thus be able to accomplish the changes we want. Often, our positions are driven by fear that we are losing our country and our only hope is a political solution.

I know some will read this and feel the need to remind me again of what is at stake. Their argument being that the other side is actively working to undermine our culture and the freedom to practice our faith. That the stakes have never been higher. I understand the argument. I am not calling for believers to be silent or accepting of things that we should not be silent about. We are clearly called to be people who seek justice and proclaim the truth.

My position is that we need to separate those things we believe as a matter of policy from the things we know are clear biblical truth. Our clearest Christian call addresses the way we conduct ourselves. The call to be different, to love our neighbor regardless of political and cultural differences, and to walk with humility and kindness is not up for political debate. Policy decisions, however, are not as clear.

While I was in office, I made a lot of decisions that were based on what I believe to be true about the world from my perspective. Sometimes those decisions pleased Republicans and those on the right side of the political spectrum. Other times, they infuriated those same folks.

The Affordable Care Act (ACA), better known as Obamacare, was passed before I came into office as governor. However, acrimony over the bill did not end with its passage. Because the bill passed with no Republican votes, pushback began instantly and continued throughout my entire time in office. Republicans sued to stop the plan, and the issue eventually rose all the way to the

US Supreme Court. The Republican challenge was based on the idea that it was not legal for the federal government to force people to buy insurance, one of the basic tenets of the Obamacare plan. The Court came back with a ruling that surprised almost everyone: the ACA was constitutional, and the federal government could require people to buy insurance. What was not constitutional, the Court ruled, was for the federal government to force states to expand who was covered by Medicaid.

Prior to the passage of the ACA, Medicaid was primarily designed to cover the disabled, children, pregnant women, and some other limited members of the households of each of those classifications. The ACA expanded Medicaid to cover everyone up to 138 percent of the federal poverty level. Because states typically paid about one-third of the cost of Medicaid, with the federal government picking up the other two-thirds, this expansion of coverage meant an expansion of costs to the states. The Court ruled that the federal government could not do that without the states' consent.

This meant that it was up to every state to decide whether they were going to expand Medicaid coverage to the new population that the ACA proposed to cover. At the time, the ACA and President Obama were very unpopular in Tennessee. Tea Party and other conservative groups held rallies and lobbied strongly against Tennessee expanding who we covered through TennCare, our version of Medicaid.

I was not a fan of the ACA. I didn't like the fact that this was passed with only Democrat votes and had very little bipartisan input in the final plan, even though it would be a major change in health care and would likely be very hard to change once it was put in place. I also did not like the fact that, while we were addressing the problem of access to health care for low-income

Americans, we did nothing to address the growing problem of the high cost of health care. I strongly believe that access to care and the cost of care are both critical issues, and both needed to be addressed.

It is a biblical truth that God has a clear concern for the least of these. There is no way to read Scripture and not come away with an overwhelming sense of God's strong concern for the poor. The policy decision, on the other hand, was not as clear. My opinion was that we were missing a big opportunity as a country by not addressing the soaring cost of health care while adding needed health-care coverage for so many. If there was ever a time to negotiate cost structure with the health-care industry, it was when we were agreeing to take over the cost of indigent health care that health-care providers had been bearing on their own. Not addressing the cost of health care would only add to our country's deficit, which meant borrowing money from future generations to pay for the cost of services provided to this generation.

In the end, I decided to make a proposal for Tennessee to expand Medicaid coverage to the low-income population. Our proposal contained elements we felt would help control health-care costs and provide needed health care to some of our most vulnerable citizens. When we announced our plan, I cited my concern for the "least of these" as one of the reasons for supporting the expansion. I did not think then, nor do I think now, that my position was the only position that a Christian could take. But my faith was the reason I decided to move forward with the proposal.

Our proposal, known as Insure Tennessee, was defeated in the legislature. It was the most significant and visible defeat our team experienced on any piece of legislation for our entire eight years. It caused a lot of conservatives to question whether I was a Republican or, in their words, a RINO (Republican in name only). Since it was such a visible defeat, I have frequently been asked if I regretted making the proposal. The answer has always been no—we truly felt it was the right thing to do.

THINKING BIBLICALLY ABOUT OUR POLITICS OR POLITICALLY ABOUT OUR FAITH

In *Mere Christianity*, C. S. Lewis points out that God reveals political ends in the Bible, but he is not as specific about the means to achieve those ends. We are supposed to feed the hungry, but we are not told how we should provide the meal. We are supposed to pursue justice, provide for widows and orphans, and fight oppression, but we are not told about the best form of government to do all of that.

This is why Lewis warned against trying to establish a Christian political party or to say any party represented the Christian position. His fear was, if that happened, you would have a political party with basic disagreements on key policy issues, or there would be a group of Christians maintaining that they represent all Christians on matters on which the Bible is not clear.[4]

Our challenge is to think biblically about our politics rather than thinking politically about our faith. That is growing more and more difficult in today's politics that are driven by passionate outrage.

About two weeks before I was sworn in as governor, I went to visit my predecessor, Phil Bredesen. We sat in his office, which was soon to become my office, amid the packing boxes and last working papers of his eight-year term. I was there to get any advice he wanted to give me as we prepared to take his place.

His advice was ageless: "The governor should do those things that only the governor can do."

As governor, you face an endless list of people and issues competing for your time. Every week we had a scheduling meeting where our scheduling team brought me a notebook full of requests for meetings. In addition to the myriad requests to speak or attend an event, there were legislators to meet with, communities to visit, businesses to recruit, forty thousand state employees to lead, and in-office meeting requests to consider. Deciding how to use the limited amount of time is one of the most difficult challenges for anyone in elected office. That is why Governor Bredesen's advice to me was so good. It is incredibly easy to fill up your calendar and agenda with things other people feel you should do but which don't really help advance your purposes.

Similarly, the church should seize this time to be about the things that only the church can do. Nathan Hatch, the president of Wake Forest University, said, "This is the opportunity—for the church to be the church, to return to the task of religious and moral formation, to build communities that bind people together, to instill a deep conviction that life can actually have transcendent purpose and is not all about individual wants and desires, and to fuel a life in which that transcendent purpose radiates into the world at large."[5]

HOW CAN THE CHURCH BE THE CHURCH IN THE POLITICAL SQUARE?

So how can the church be the church? We can realize that our battle is not with people who disagree with us politically or with the culture that seems to be against us. Our battle is to bring meaning and love to a world struggling with meaninglessness and despair in a way that has rarely been seen. Today's climate of meaninglessness is so severe that a new term, "deaths of despair," has been coined to describe the mounting numbers of deaths due to suicide, alcoholism, or drug overdose.[6] Drug overdose deaths are increasing. College campuses are dealing with what is almost an epidemic of depression. Fewer and fewer people report having more than one or two close friends.[7] Our world increasingly longs for the words of grace and truth that only the church can give.

I believe every Christian is called to be in the public square in some way. Maybe it is in elected office, or it could be to serve as an informed and caring citizen and voter. In a later chapter, I will talk about how much we would be weakened as communities and as a nation without the faithful presence of believers. But the danger comes when those believers see their faith as a means to bring about the political ends they want.

The church, the body of believers, has a key role in the political process. But that role has to be marked by humility and reflection. It also has to be marked by a commitment to be more faithful to the Word of God than we are to either political party. In the words of Gary Haugen, founder of International Justice Mission, the church should be using our influence to "bless the world out of love rather than cursing the world out of fear."

When it comes to the public square, the church has to move from a fear of what we are losing to a deep desire to share the "hope that is in [us]" (1 Peter 3:15).

4

WHY SHOULD WE CARE ABOUT THE PUBLIC GOOD?

We should ask the next natural question before moving on: Should a believer even have a presence in the public square? Wouldn't it be better to focus on growing the church and leave the messiness of politics to others? After all, as Paul reminds us in Philippians, "Our citizenship is in heaven, and from it we await a Savior" (3:20), and Hebrews tells us, "Here we have no lasting city, but we seek the city that is to come" (13:14).

The argument is that Jesus never got involved in politics. He ignored Herod, Pilate, and every other political person, so why should we get involved? He was clear that his kingdom was not of this world.

Many Christians fear getting involved because they sense that, whether you are a candidate or just involved in the political process, it is all too manipulative, dirty, and full of narcissists. Besides, it often means giving up a world of black-and-white choices for a world where your choices are between gray and grayer.

I understand the sentiment. Having run for office on multiple occasions and having been a mayor and governor for fifteen years, I know that campaigns are personal and difficult at best. When I was running for governor the first time in 2010, I announced my candidacy in January the year prior. This meant that the campaign lasted almost two years, about as long as the nervous pit in my stomach lasted.

We had a very competitive Republican primary with four legitimate candidates. One of the hallmarks of a statewide campaign is county-level political party dinners. Republicans call them Lincoln Day or Reagan Day dinners. Democrats would call their events either Jackson Day or Truman Day dinners. They usually draw only the most committed, intense party members.

Tennessee has ninety-five counties, which means that there are that many opportunities for each county's Republican Party to have a dinner every year. You'd better have a good excuse if you are going to miss one. Our campaign lasted almost two years, so we attended dinners in many of the counties twice. Because all the candidates usually attend, as well as their most passionate local supporters, the dinners were sometimes awkward and occasionally worse. There was always a time for each candidate to give a speech. By the end of the campaign, we had heard one another so much that we could give the others' speeches. Multiple candidates, their most passionate supporters, cold buffet food, and a small room could make for a long night. Crissy would always come with me, and occasionally one of our children would attend as well. After one of the events in a crowded room with heated speeches that lasted for hours on a hot summer night, my daughter Leigh told me, "Daddy, I love you, and I really want you to win. But please don't ask me to do that again." I knew how she felt.

I can also still remember the moment I saw the first negative television ad that an opponent ran against me. I was standing in the doorway between our bedroom and bathroom, brushing my teeth and watching the late news before bed. Suddenly, a grainy black-and-white picture of me came on the screen. As the narrator spoke in an ominous tone, all sorts of reasons not to vote for me came rolling across the screen. It stuck in my gut, but Crissy laughed and said, "Now that I know what you are really like, I am not sure if I can stay in the same house with you tonight." Whereupon she rolled over and went to sleep. It took me a little longer to close my eyes and go to sleep. Running for public office is not a decision to be made lightly. While campaigning is a lot about generating sound bites and summarizing your position, governing is more complex.

Though I like the governing part a lot better than the campaigning part, governing is far from easy. The reality of making decisions is complicated by the fact that sometimes there is not a perfectly pure answer. Frequently a leader's choices are not clear-cut, even when you are trying to do the right thing. For instance, when you have to balance a budget, and you have a limited amount of revenue, you are inevitably choosing between good and worthy alternatives. Pay teachers more or hire more prison guards? Provide more services to the disabled citizens you are already covering or cover more disabled citizens?

What campaigning and governing have in common is that they are both a contact sport. I know what it feels like to be on one end of an issues battle where the other side has unleashed a full-scale social media barrage. Or to wake up in the morning to a news story that seems totally unfair, and that questions not only your decisions but also your motives.

This is what happened to me on Mother's Day 2013. I had decided to get up early to cook and celebrate Crissy by bringing her breakfast in bed. (Full disclosure: this was a pretty rare occurrence.) As I scrambled eggs, I glanced over at the newspaper one of the state troopers who manned the security station in a building next to the house had left on the counter. The bold headline on the front page above the fold (placement of an article used to matter when most people read a physical copy of the paper) screamed HASLAM DOES SECRET DEAL TO AID PARTNER. I quickly grabbed the paper since I had no idea what they could be talking about.

Turns out, someone with whom I had been a minority partner in a real estate deal years earlier had gotten a bill passed in the legislature to allow him to open up a tourist-oriented distillery in the resort town of Gatlinburg. About 2,500 bills are proposed by the legislature every year. On each one, our team as the executive branch would declare our position—"support," "oppose," or "defer to the will of the legislature"—before the bill began its journey through the legislature. The last category meant that we would not be engaging in the legislative debate about the bill in any way. Our role would be only to sign the bill if it passed. I had never discussed this particular bill with the sponsor or anyone else, and I was not even aware of who was involved.

This was one of the many bills we deferred on every year that was passed by the legislature. Like most of the bills that we deferred on, I did not pay much attention when it came to my desk along with scores of other bills to be signed. However, if you read the paper, it was easy to believe that I had worked to help my business associate pass his bill and then secretly signed it without disclosing that he was my business partner, with the obvious inference that I would benefit from the arrangement.

Needless to say, Crissy's scrambled eggs were cold when I finally got them upstairs. In the meantime, I had called the editor of the paper, who was not expecting to get a call from the governor as her Happy Mother's Day good morning. The reporter who wrote the story, far from being apologetic, was mainly upset that his editor was waking him up at 9:00 a.m. on a Sunday. As for me, I walked into church that morning pretty sure that everyone was thinking I was a crook.

It does seem purer sometimes, not to mention easier, to just separate from the whole political situation.

There were times when the attacks felt relentless and unfair.

There were times when it felt like the media would never let up on whatever they were hounding me about, and every morning brought another news cycle rehashing whatever they had blasted me for the day before.

During one of those times, I asked John Wood, who was then the pastor of our church in Knoxville, how he handled criticisms from his congregation. He replied, "No matter what they say about me, I always remind myself, they don't know the half of it. There are many more reasons than that to be critical of me." While that is hard to live out when you feel like a fish being fired on in a barrel, it does reflect an accurate view of what it would look like if everyone could see everyone else's motives, thoughts, and hidden actions.

The reality about leadership is that when we step forward, we are opening ourselves up to fair and unfair opinions. If the only Christians willing to lead are the ones who actually enjoy tension and conflict for the sake of the limelight, the church will certainly be misrepresented. Leadership is a vulnerable profession whether in business, church, or government. But lead we must.

EXERCISING REASON IN THE
SHADOWY REALMS

Are moral ambiguity and personal vulnerability reasons for us to avoid the public square? Is it not better to stick to safe places where we will not have to worry about the morally perilous areas of politics? Far from it. It is that ambiguity and difficulty that makes it so important for believers to enter into the process. Martin Luther said, "The very ablest youth should be reserved and educated, not for the office of preaching, but for the government. Because in preaching the Holy Spirit does it all, whereas in government one must exercise reason in the shadowy realms where ambiguity and uncertainty are the orders of the day."[1]

It is precisely because the public square is such a morally perilous place that believers should not exempt themselves from the arena. Our founders never contemplated a country where religious people were not intimately involved in its governance. John Adams wrote that "our Constitution was made only for a moral and religious people. It is wholly inadequate to the government of any other."[2]

Perhaps the unique role of people of faith can be as citizens who realize that our nation's story is not about us in a world full of people who want the story to be about them. Tim Keller suggests that we can be "self-sacrificers rather than self-actualizers. Late modern secularism instills deep the notion that we should never give up our interest or rights for anyone else, we should always assert ourselves, and we should be righteously angry as we do so."[3]

But that is not what we are called to be. Our call is never about self-actualization; it is never about being "my best me." Our call is to lead more like Jesus. Servant leadership has become a common phrase in conversations about effective leadership. But we follow One who was a servant leader long before it was cool to be a servant leader: "The Son of Man came not to be served but to serve, and to give his life as a ransom for many" (Matthew 20:28). So as Christians, our call to be a faithful presence in the public arena, and everywhere else for that matter, always starts with self-sacrifice—not self-actualization. For while Christians know that the story is not about us, we also have the confidence that comes from knowing that we are part of a bigger story that God is writing.

THE ROLE OF GOVERNMENT

In the coming pages, I want to talk about how we must live as part of the bigger story that God is writing in this divided and weary country. One of the difficulties of living in a pluralistic society like ours is that there is no consensus on government's role or purpose. Frequently, people will ask me about the difference between leading a government and leading a business. To me, the biggest difference is that in a business, everyone agrees on the purpose of the business. If you are manufacturing widgets, you want to manufacture and sell as many high-quality widgets as the market will demand. In a well-run company, the workforce, leadership, and board are all unified in the purpose and mission of the business.

That is not true in a government. In government, there are almost as many visions for what the government should do and be as there are citizens. Often, leadership in government means balancing competing valid interests. It also means leading in a world where people have a wide variety of opinions on how active government should be and how much it should require in taxes. Government provides services—interstate highways, armies, schools, and hundreds of other things—in exchange for the taxes its citizens pay. I always felt like one of my prime responsibilities as a mayor or governor was to make certain that we gave the very best services we could for the very lowest price in taxes. While hot-button political issues tend to draw all the attention during a campaign, I always felt I was in the job to make certain that we served people well.

Leaving office gives you a different perspective. I will long remember the inauguration day of my successor, Bill Lee. First, it is a pretty remarkable feeling to lose that much power so fast! You are governor until the moment you are not. One minute you are in charge of a state with forty thousand employees and a $37 billion budget. You can call out the National Guard to respond to emergencies, appoint judges, grant pardons, release prisoners, name university board members, and even perform wedding ceremonies. The next minute you are the guy who used to be governor. As the Australians say, "rooster today, feather duster tomorrow."

Right after the ceremony, one of our legislators, whom I had worked with for eight years, came up holding his phone and said he wanted a picture with the governor. I said sure and prepared to pose with him when instead he handed me the phone and went to stand by Governor Lee so I could take their picture. Having had my new reality so clearly illustrated, Crissy and I got in our car and, after eight years of being driven by state troopers, tried to remember the rules of the road as we drove home to Knoxville.

When you are out of office, people tend to ask you what your biggest surprise was about being governor. My answer, then and now, is that I was surprised at what a big deal it is to be governor. I hadn't realized that when you showed up in a small town, the whole town might come out to meet you. Living in the Governor's Residence, working in a historic state capitol, and going to state dinners at the White House were certainly not my experience before I was in office. But that is not what I meant. The surprise to me was in how much difference a governor or a mayor can make.

Before I was in office, I totally underestimated the impact of the office. Being in a public role gave me the chance to serve in a way that I had not anticipated. The truth is, being involved in the public arena gives us a chance to leverage our opportunities for change in a way that is difficult outside a public service role. What is decided through the political process and how it gets decided matter a great deal because those decisions affect so many people. And how to effectively deliver the services it is entrusted to deliver is just as important as the decisions that are made in the political process. That is why we should all care about who we elect and who serves us in public roles.

Of course, I do not believe that every person who reads this book should run for office. But I do believe everyone is called to serve the common good. This means that each of you will be criticized, sometimes unfairly, for the stands you take and the decisions you make. But it also means you have the opportunity to be different, to be light in a world that has lost its way.

Why should we care about the common good? Why should we enter the dangerous public square? Because it matters who we elect and whether the folks in the public square are there to serve or to be served. And because God asked us to be a part of cultivating the garden (Genesis 2:15). And because God "makes his sun rise on the evil and on the good, and sends rain on the just and on the unjust" (Matthew 5:45). And because "God so loved the world . . ." (John 3:16).

5

IF THE MEEK WILL INHERIT THE EARTH, WHO WILL RUN FOR OFFICE?

It has been said that those who choose to seek the high road of humility in politics will never run into a traffic jam. There is more than a little bit of truth in that statement. A friend of mine used to tell me that politics was for people who wanted to be in show business but didn't have the looks. Might be a little truth there too.

There is no doubt that politics attracts more than its fair share of oversized egos. Some of that is due to the filtering process of being a candidate. After all, it takes a certain amount of confidence to run for office. You are saying, "I am here for you to evaluate me." At times it feels like a cattle call.

The candidate, like the cow being auctioned, is brought on the stage to be looked over, poked, and compared while voters decide if he or she is worthy. If you've decided to run for office, you are now open to the comments and critiques of anyone who cares to weigh in. If you're really unlucky, you will also have an opponent who chooses to spend a lot of money on television to let everyone know that you are too liberal, too conservative, crooked, a puppet, inexperienced, and that you hate children and old people.

Like being a cornerback in the NFL or an actor on Broadway, being in political office requires the confidence to do your job in front of an audience, many of whom are hoping you will fail. Running for office also requires the confidence that you will win the election. During Donald Trump's inauguration in January 2017, as at all inaugurations, all the governors were seated on the podium behind the president. The new president and vice president were joined by the former president and vice president, along with the incoming cabinet, Congress, the Supreme Court, other assorted dignitaries, and a crowd stretching from the US Capitol back toward the Washington Monument. This inauguration was interesting, not just for the usual reason of the new leader and the retiring president sharing a stage but because it also meant that Donald Trump and Hillary Clinton would be together for the first time since their election contest.

I was sitting between two governors who had also been candidates for president in the Republican primary. Scott Walker, the governor of Wisconsin, was on my left, and Chris Christie, the governor of New Jersey, was on my right. Scott leaned across me and said, "Chris, I don't know about you, but I was hoping for a different seat at this event." Before Chris could respond, John Kasich, the governor of Ohio and another primary contestant, who happened to be sitting in front of me, leaned back and said, "I know just how you feel."

Running for office not only requires a certain amount of confidence, it also usually includes the disorienting experience of starring in your own commercials. In those commercials, the candidate is supposed to explain why he or she is the answer to all the problems of that city, state, or country. The power of advertising makes you recognizable anywhere you go. When I ran for governor in 2010, we decided to begin our television advertising earlier than usual to take advantage of the Winter Olympics airing on television. The US Olympic team was performing better than expected during the games, so television viewership was also much higher than expected. Because of that, I became better known much quicker across the state than if we had waited.

One time, when I was in a neighborhood in middle Tennessee

knocking on doors to introduce myself, a teenager answered the door and shouted back to his mother, "Hey, Mom, it's the guy from the Olympics!" I am pretty sure that's the only time I've ever been confused for an Olympic athlete.

There is always a temptation to walk in pride when you're put into a position like this; and, once elected, that temptation only increases. After I was elected governor, it seemed that my speeches got more interesting and my jokes got funnier. Your sense of self-importance swells as the list of people who want to meet with you grows and grows. You move to a big house behind the gate, and state troopers drive you everywhere you go. When you are introduced for a speech, the whole room rises to applaud as you approach the podium with the wisdom that is sure to follow.

It turns out, even your recreational activities can feed your pride when you're in office. My first year in office, I went duck hunting with my son, Will, and four other men. You should know that I am not very good with a shotgun. I always joke that I have a better chance of hitting a bird by throwing the gun than I do of downing a duck by actually shooting the gun. For those of you who are not duck hunters, it usually involves several hunters crouching in a duck blind early on a very cold morning. The idea is for the hunters to remain hidden until the birds are within range. Then, as the ducks begin to near the blind, the hunters rise and shoot. Usually there are enough birds spread out in front of the hunters that it is obvious who shot which duck. But occasionally, multiple hunters end up shooting at the same duck. On this morning, four of us rose to shoot at the lone duck that was descending in front of us. I cannot be sure, but I am almost positive that my shot missed its mark. However, when the duck fell, the entire group exclaimed, "Great shot, Governor!"

As you might imagine, it is easy to start thinking you are a big deal when you keep getting treated like you are a big deal. Whether you are on the city council or you are president of the United States, being in elected office means being treated special. From there the walk from being treated special to thinking you are special turns out to be only a few short steps.

More problematic than thinking you are special is the next short step of thinking you are always right.

HAVING ALL THE RIGHT ANSWERS

Most of us, office seekers or not, come into the public square because we have opinions about the answers to certain problems. Perhaps it is the desire to provide better health care or equal access to quality education. Maybe we are driven by our perception of the deteriorating culture of the country or a fear about a warming planet or a growing budget deficit. The issues that drive us and the passion of our convictions push us to try and solve problems. We think we have the answers, or we would not be there. Our desire to be a part of the solution is at the heart of all the good reasons we step forward. On the one hand, passion, combined with humility, provides great soil for a fruitful entry into the public square. On the other hand, misplaced passion can lead to harmful crashes in the public square.

When my children were growing up, I spent a lot of time coaching their various sports teams. I have always loved sports and enjoyed hanging around my kids and their friends, so it was a good fit. In my time watching kids' sports, I learned something about adults: sports bring out the worst in us. Otherwise mature adults would get red-faced at an umpire's mistake in a T-ball game where an inning is not over until everyone bats. I was guilty of that a few times myself.

Politics is the same way. Passions can become inflamed in what may have started as a casual discussion with friends or neighbors. Because we know we have the right answer, it is frustrating when others cannot see it our way. And like overzealous parents watching a T-ball game, it often brings out the worst in us.

What would our political conversations look like if we started every one by imitating Peter and James and reminding ourselves to be humble? How different would it be if we were known as much for our humility as we are for our political stances?

ALWAYS REMEMBER, THE OTHER PERSON JUST MAY BE RIGHT

My first job in politics was serving as an intern for Senator Howard Baker in Washington, DC. I was a college student who was pretty sure he was coming to Washington to help save the republic. Instead, my job looked more like answering constituent letters in those pre-email days and taking messages to the chief of staff in those pre–cell phone days.

While my role was not quite what I envisioned on my drive from Tennessee to DC, I learned a lifetime of lessons about political service from Senator Baker. When he was elected to the US Senate in 1966, he became the first Republican elected to the senate in Tennessee in ninety years. He would go on to become the Senate Majority Leader, serve as President Reagan's chief of staff, and be appointed US ambassador to Japan. Senator Baker was from Scott County, a rural area just north of Knoxville. What

I most remember was his admonition to "always remember, the other fella might be right."

That advice seems almost quaint or naive today. I know words like that cause many Christians to say, "That all sounds nice, but that is not the world we live in today. Today the values we believe in are under attack by elites with a secular mindset. This is a battle for the soul of America, and we cannot unilaterally disarm and play nice when the other side surely will not do that. The stakes are too high, and besides, politics has never been for the fainthearted."

I am not arguing that we should always find the middle spot, to simply find a compromise position that allows us to move on from the sticky problem. If we do not hold certain convictions—things we know to be true or right regardless of circumstance—there is no reason to be engaged in public policy. We do not need any more elected officials who really don't have any convictions beyond getting reelected.

What I am arguing is that we should remember why we came into the public square in the first place. We are there because we think the decisions made by our elected leaders truly do impact the peace of the city where we have been called. We believe that good government is one of the key things that influences the health of our communities, states, and country. We also believe that getting to the *right* answer is more important than just getting to *our* answer. And so it would be wise to remember Senator Baker's admonition and to keep in mind that we are not all-knowing or infallible.

The most life-changing truth about being a Christian is understanding our own brokenness. Everything I am saying about humility and our sense of who we are and how we fit into this grand political scheme is based on this truth. When we forget this truth, we find ourselves with problems we face today. If there is one thing Christians should be known for in the public square, it is humility. Or, put another way, if there is one thing we should *not* be known for, it is pride. Of all the sins we focus on and hope to erase from our lives and our communities, pride should be at the top of the list.

C. S. Lewis put it this way: "According to Christian teachers, the essential vice, the utmost evil, is Pride. Unchastity, anger, greed, drunkenness, and all that, are mere fleabites in comparison: it was through Pride that the devil became the devil: Pride leads to every other vice: it is the complete anti-God state of mind."[1]

It is serious language to claim that the sins we tend to focus on, like sins of sexuality and drunkenness, are only fleabites compared to pride—and that pride leads to all the other sins. Yet that is what Scripture teaches. Other than the accounts of Jesus' life in the Gospels, the New Testament writers rarely repeated one another word for word. The notable exception to that is in letters written by two of the people who knew Jesus best. Peter, one of the disciples closest to Jesus, and James, Jesus' brother, both used the exact same blunt words to tell us that "God opposes the proud but gives grace to the humble" (1 Peter 5:5; James 4:6).

In the words of Jack Miller, "Cheer up; you're a lot worse off than you think you are, but in Jesus you're far more loved than you could have ever imagined."[2] While I love the part of God loving me more than I could ever imagine, I also know the reality of the part that says I am worse than I think, that I am more selfish and sinful than I want to admit—to myself or to you. Paul put it this way in Romans: "All have sinned and fall short of the glory of God" (3:23). The *Book of Common Prayer* expresses it this way: "We have followed too much the devices and desires of our own hearts."[3]

If we truly believe that, we know we never have the right to be self-righteous or condescending or disdainful of others' opinions in public debate or anywhere else. A true understanding of our own shortcomings and failings should lead us to always start from a position of humility.

WHAT ARE WE KNOWN FOR?

Are Christians in the public square known for our humility as much as we are known for our position on certain issues?

If we prioritized what we talked and prayed about—and what we look for in our leaders—by how frequently Scripture speaks about humility, our political conversations and convictions would be dramatically different. If we based our words on the words in Scripture, then most of our political discussions would include the danger of pride and the beauty of humility. By my count, *pride* or one of its varieties (e.g., *conceit, boasting, vanity,* etc.) is mentioned almost three hundred times in the Bible, without counting the many times it is the main point of a story or parable. *Humility* and its variations come up more than 250 times in the Old and New Testament. Given that, should not our humility be how we are known?

If you asked most people today what defines Christians in the public square, I am pretty sure their answers would include the issues of abortion, gay marriage, religious freedom, and selecting judges who would protect the traditional view on each of these issues. For most Americans today, the word *evangelical* describes a voting block of primarily conservative Republican voters who are known for their advocacy on these issues.

This is not an argument against the position Christians have held on these issues for two thousand years. As we will discuss later, while I was in office, I took stands against abortion and in favor of traditional marriage and the freedom to live in a way that we can be true to our religious convictions. All those issues are important and should not be ignored. My question here, though, is this: Shouldn't Christians be known for our humility as much as we are for our position on those issues?

MEEKNESS: WHAT IS IT—REALLY?

In Matthew 5, Jesus said, "Blessed are the meek, for they shall inherit the earth" (v. 5). But meekness is not exactly the most desirable trait these days, is it? Today we hear the word *meek* and think *timid* and *shy*. But we know that is not what Jesus meant by meek because we are also reminded in Scripture that we are not to be timid. Paul told Timothy, the one he described as his beloved child, "The Spirit God gave us does not make us timid, but gives us power, love and self-discipline" (2 Timothy 1:7 NIV). So what exactly does it mean, then, to be meek in our approach to the public square?

As D. Martyn Lloyd-Jones said in *Studies in the Sermon on the Mount*, "Meekness is essentially a true view of oneself, expressing itself in attitude and conduct with respect to others. . . . The man who is truly meek is the one who is truly amazed that God and man can think of him as well as they do and treat him as well as they do."[4]

It also might help to remember where Jesus placed "blessed are the meek" in the Sermon on the Mount. It seems significant that it is right between those who mourn over sin and those who hunger and thirst for righteousness. We are quick to crusade

67

against evil or unrighteousness when we see it. The meekness that Jesus asks of us, though, requires a sorrow for our own brokenness before we pursue righteousness for ourselves, our neighbors, our state, and our country. The reality is, others are much more likely to listen to our plea for a more righteous society if we begin with the recognition of our own failings.

While humility has never been easy, it seems to be even harder today when humility has gone out of style—and not just in politics. NFL receivers celebrate a seven-yard completion for a first down like they just caught the winning touchdown in the Super Bowl. Business leaders write books about themselves and their remarkable achievements. Entertainers demand that concert promoters stock their dressing rooms with a very specific menu, such as a bowl of M&M'S without any green ones or only green ones.

Pride and protecting one's pride, however, are very much in fashion. All of us want to be right in every argument and look good in every situation. But of course, pride comes before the fall—sometimes literally, as I learned on live television.

I was attending a morning meeting of governors at the White House. As the meeting concluded, I was asked if I would join a small group of governors to meet with the media. I agreed, and soon four other governors and I were headed out the front door of the White House and over to the front of the West Wing, where a bank of microphones and accompanying cameras awaited.

You have seen the scene hundreds of times on the news when someone emerges from the White House and stops to address the media. ABC, CBS, NBC, Fox, CNN, MSNBC, BBC, and other news organizations were all represented. As the saying goes, there is no more dangerous place in the world than the space between a politician and a camera, so we were all moving at a pretty good clip.

As we neared the microphones, I glanced up to see if I recognized anyone in the media group. The next thing I knew, I was face down on the pavement. I had not seen a piece of equipment that a camera man had left on the ground. I did not just trip. I fell. Hard. In front of the cameras of almost every large media organization in the country. This was not one of those falls where you catch yourself on the way down and maybe leave a rip in your pants at the knee. This was one of those falls where you go down so fast that you hit your chin.

My first thought was to roll over, get up, and walk toward the White House gate as fast as I could. But then I decided that would not be very professional, so I picked the rocks out of my palms, dusted myself off, and joined the other governors at the microphones. Two of the governors had horrified looks on their faces and whispered, "Did you hurt anything?"

"Only my pride," I whispered back. While my pride was hurt, this was a good moment for me to remember why I was there. And perhaps it was a reminder from God. I was not there to be important or to feel powerful. I was there to bless, not impress. Nothing like a belly flop on the pavement to stir you out of a sense of self-importance.

A MISSED CHANCE TO ASK FORGIVENESS

After I left the governor's office, I became the board chair of Young Life, a ministry to middle and high school students in 185 countries around the world. Crissy and I were visiting Africa to see Young Life in action in Tanzania and Rwanda.

One afternoon we were visiting the former sight of a slave market in Zanzibar, one of the last open slave markets until it was shut down in 1873. It was to this coastal market that as many as five hundred thousand Africans were brought every year after being seized from their homes and villages. From there, they were shipped to other countries, including ours. Underneath the building stood the small, dark cells where captured slaves were kept before being sold. I could barely stand to be in one of the rooms for a few minutes with a few people and could not fathom the horror of being stuffed in there with hundreds of others for a long time.

After slavery ended, the market became a church. The former site of the trading block became an altar, and the pit where the bodies of children were discarded was now the site of the baptismal font. Today, the building stands as a monument and reminder of the horrors of the slave trade. Guides tell the story of the atrocities that happened there. We were sitting in the former slave-market-turned-church, listening to one of those guides, when someone tapped me on the shoulder.

"Excuse me. Are you Bill Haslam?" Startled, I replied that I was. "Well, there is a group of African American mayors from the United States here, and they recognized you and wanted to know if they could have a picture with you." I said I would be glad to and walked over to where they were gathered.

One of the people with me was Alexis Kwamy, who grew up in the Congo and is now the Young Life vice president of Africa South.

After we had taken the picture, Alexis asked if he could speak for a minute. He then asked for forgiveness. He said that his African ancestors had kidnapped these African American mayors' ancestors and sold them to slave traders. While technically that might not have been true, Alexis confessed that many

Africans had been on the front end of the slave trade, and on behalf of a lot of people who looked like him, he was asking for their forgiveness. He spoke of the horrible consequences of sinful behavior and the beauty of a grace that forgives. Crissy and I were both near tears as we listened to Alexis speak with humility and sorrow about what had happened.

And I'm sad to say that I missed it. I missed the chance to add my confession to what Alexis had said. I missed the chance to add my confession on behalf of a lot of people who looked like me and had perpetuated slavery in America. I am not aware of any slaveholders in my family, but standing there, I did have the chance to apologize for the centuries of mistreatment of black people by white people. Alexis's words stood in stark contrast to my silence. His humility offset my pride.

ERNIE PYLE AND DWIGHT EISENHOWER

In his book *The Road to Character*, David Brooks writes about listening to the rebroadcast of a radio show called *Command Performance*, a variety show for the troops during World War II.

> The episode I happened to hear was broadcast the day after V-J day, on August 15, 1945.
>
> The episode featured some of the era's biggest celebrities: Frank Sinatra, Marlene Dietrich, Cary Grant, Bette Davis, and many others. But the most striking feature of the show was its tone of self-effacement and humility. The Allies had just completed one of the noblest military victories in human history. And yet there was no chest beating. Nobody was erecting triumphal arches.[5]

Brooks goes on to describe the program and how the host, Bing Crosby, summarized the mood with, "Today . . . our deep-down feeling is one of humility."[6]

The program also included a reading of an article written by Ernie Pyle, the famous war correspondent who had been killed a few months before the end of the war. Anticipating the victory, he had already written these words: "We won the war because our men are brave and because of many other things—because of Russia, England, and China and the passage of time and the gift of nature's materials. We did not win it because destiny created us better than all other people. I hope that in victory we are more grateful than proud."[7]

I cannot help but compare that to the T-shirt I recently saw on a man at the beach seventy years after the conclusion of the war, proclaiming the United States as "Back-to-Back World Champs," referring to World Wars I and II.

In a world that has lost its taste for humility, shouldn't we be the people who model a humble approach to the public square? We are, after all, the people who should understand grace. And understanding grace means that, at our core, we know we are not better than other people. We have no reason to walk into the public square with an attitude of self-righteousness. I know it seems backward, but the more we humble ourselves, the more fruit God promises, even in a world that has lost its taste for humility.

I'm reminded of a story about Dwight Eisenhower, who was the supreme commander of Allied forces during World War II. It was his responsibility to make the final decision to launch the invasion of Normandy. Hanging in the balance were the lives of thousands of soldiers as well as the outcome of the war. More than seventy-five years later, we know the decision to move forward was obviously the right one. But at the time, deteriorating weather conditions meant that Allied airplanes could not take off and Allied forces would not have the air cover they were expecting.

Prior to the launch, Eisenhower wrote a letter that, thankfully, he never had to send. He had prepared a memo in case the momentous D-day landing at Normandy failed.

> Our landings . . . have failed . . . and I have withdrawn the troops. My decision to attack at this time and place was based upon the best information available. The troops, the air and the Navy did all that bravery and devotion could do. If any blame or fault attaches to the attempt it is mine alone.[8]

Most of us would have too much pride to write that letter. Instead, we would look for a way to spin the story to protect our pride and reputation. Think how exceedingly rare it is for a leader today to say, "I am sorry. I did not get that one right."

This only drives home the point that as Christians in the public square, and everywhere else for that matter, we should be known for humility as much or more than we are known for our positions. To lack humility is to misunderstand the gospel. "God opposes the proud but gives grace to the humble" (James 4:6).

6

IS IT HARD TO BE A CHRISTIAN IN POLITICS?

So just how hard is it to be a Christian in politics and government?

People often ask me that question. When they do, I typically respond, "Oh, I am not sure it is that much more difficult than doing anything else. What makes you say that about politics?" Their reply usually falls into a couple of categories. The first is a perception that is probably a result of watching too many television shows and Netflix series on politics. As nasty as politics can be, it is not *that* nasty. So, while it isn't a lot of fun to watch a negative commercial about yourself from an opponent's campaign—and I haven't missed being blistered by comments on Facebook or having a legislator say one thing and do another—the good people in politics far outweigh the bad, and the rewards are far greater than the challenges.

The second reason people ask about the difficulty of being a Christian in politics is the observation that people of faith face discrimination or persecution because of their faith. While that is true in some places and at some times, this, too, is not as difficult as many assume. In fact, the temptation more often is to use your faith to score political points—to use God instead of being used by God.

So, for me, walking into the morally treacherous waters of politics was not the hard part. And, braving the consequences of being identified as a Christian was not the heart of the challenge. The real challenge in politics, just like the challenge in every other endeavor, is to live out what we say we believe. Perhaps it is harder in public office because the role is so much more visible, but the challenge is the same for all of us. You do not have to spend too much time reading the New Testament to find several verses that will leave you asking, How can I possibly do that in this job?

While there are many ways in which living out the words of the New Testament is difficult, especially in a public role, three particular areas stand out to me. Let's take some time to do a deep dive into each of them.

ANXIETY

Because politics is such a high stakes, visible endeavor, it would be hard to be involved without being challenged by Paul's instruction in Philippians: "Do not be anxious about anything, but in everything by prayer and supplication with thanksgiving let your requests be made known to God. And the peace of God, which surpasses all understanding, will guard your hearts and your minds in Christ Jesus" (4:6–7). Some people might be able to run as a candidate in a competitive political race and find it easy to be anxious for nothing, but I am not one of them.

Before running for mayor and governor, I spent a long period of time talking with people throughout the city and the state about the opportunity. I loved those conversations. I loved meeting people, asking questions, and gaining insight that would help me if I had the chance to serve in office. For me, the period of time between exploring the possibility of running and actually announcing that I was going to run was an interesting adventure. But once I actually announced that I was running, the entire experience changed from a learning adventure to an intense challenge.

Until you have actually been a candidate, it is hard to describe the vulnerability of running for office. The first time Ronald Reagan ran for governor of California in 1966, he said it was "like stepping off the high dive and realizing you were on the way to the water and it might be cold." When you raise your hand and say, "I want to represent you," everything changes. You become a salesman with yourself as the product. Some people enjoy that, but I had to work at being comfortable in that role.

There are parts of the campaign I truly enjoyed. I really do like learning more about issues and understanding the arguments for and against particular ideas. I also like the personal interaction of meeting people and hearing their concerns. Unlike some candidates, I liked the part of campaigning known as "door knocking." When you add together the two different times I ran for mayor and my two campaigns for governor, I knocked on more than ten thousand doors and then stood on front porches and introduced myself and explained why I was running. You learn a lot about people while standing on their front porch, including the reality that what people are really concerned about is rarely whatever is dominating the news at that point.

I also loved putting together a team to work on the campaign and developing a strategy that would guide the effort. Many of the people who joined our campaign team in 2009 were recent college graduates adjusting to their first real job. When we left office almost ten years later, most were married with kids, and we had been able to walk with them through our political challenges and their new stages of life. This sense of communal effort was both a joy and a source of stress in some ways.

Some of my anxiety was due to the fact that I knew I was not the only one invested in the effort. A great campaign involves not just a great campaign staff but hundreds of volunteers who join in to help. It also means a lot of people make endorsements, donate financial gifts, host events, and contribute in other ways toward victory. As the campaign progresses, you feel more and more of a sense that you do not want to let down the folks who have stuck out their necks for you. Most of all, your family is in the campaign as well. And the campaign often feels more personal and difficult for the spouse and other family members than it does for the candidate.

The Family on the Campaign Trail

Before I ran for mayor the first time in 2003, Crissy and I gathered our children together to get their feedback on how they felt about me running for office. Our son, Will, was a high school senior at that time. After hearing the plan, he said, "I will be away in college by the time the election happens. It won't affect me as much as it would if I were younger, so do whatever you think is the right thing to do."

Annie was a sophomore in high school at the time and would be a junior when the election was held. She asked us the reasons for running and the reasons that would make us decide not to run. After hearing both, she said that all of our reasons not to run—we might lose, opponents could say negative things about us, and it would be a lot of work—sounded selfish, and she thought we should go for it. Our youngest daughter, Leigh, was in eighth grade at the time and expressed the view of all eighth graders: "Just don't lose or do anything else to embarrass me."

Leigh's middle school honesty goes a long way toward explaining the anxiety I felt despite Paul's words to the Philippians—and to all of us—to be anxious for nothing. Running for office is highly visible. This is not a job you get to do in the privacy and comfort of your own home or office. Everything you say and do is on a public stage, and eventually you will say something you wish you had not said. I know very few first-time candidates who don't at some point ask themselves, *What was I thinking?* Running for office is not only highly visible, it is also a high-stakes endeavor. There are no consolation positions or prizes for coming in second. Either you win and go into office or you lose and go home.

BATTLING ANXIETIES

As much as I hate to admit it, I felt that anxiety during both my first-term campaigns for mayor and governor. I can clearly remember the night about two weeks before my first election in 2003. A friend of mine, Steve Chesney, called and asked if he could drop by for a few minutes. After a bit of small talk, he looked at me and asked, "You know it is going to be okay, don't you?"

I am sure I looked back at him with confusion, since I was thinking, *How would he know what is going to happen in the election?* He replied, "I have no idea what is going to happen in the election. But I do know that it is still going to be okay. The same faithful God who called you to run will still be the sovereign God of the universe who means you well regardless of what happens in the voting booth." Echoing the words that Crissy had told me many times, Steve said, "Your job is to run this race in a faithful way. God will use the election to let you know if your next job will be mayor."

In my 2010 governor's race, our campaign was big enough that we used frequent polling to understand how the race was going in the weeks leading up to the election. Up until about three weeks before election day, our polls showed us with a comfortable lead of fifteen points or more. But then, one of our opponents ran a highly effective commercial featuring endorsements from several well-known figures. Every night we watched as our lead diminished by a point.

This time it was four other men who reminded me that the real issue for me should be my faithfulness rather than my diminishing lead in the polls. For the prior twenty-five years, every Friday at 6:15 a.m., these four guys had come to my house to pray and talk. That Friday morning, I reaped the benefits of those twenty-five years of sharing life with them. Those friends knew me well enough to remind me why I was running and that anxiety was not supposed to be the outcome.

HUMILITY

As difficult as it is to not be anxious in a highly visible, high-stakes political world, I have found another instruction Paul gives in Philippians even more difficult. We've talked about how rare humility is in the public arena, but Philippians 2:3–4 always seemed particularly challenging when I was campaigning: "Do nothing from selfish ambition or conceit, but in humility count others more significant than yourselves. Let each of you look not only to his own interests, but also to the interests of others." I dare you to find a campaign consultant who would give you that advice. Campaigns are all about saying, "I am the man or woman who can solve the problems that our city, state, or country is facing. Elect me because I will be a much better leader than any of these other people I am running against." That sounds a long way from doing nothing from selfish ambition or conceit and counting others more significant than yourself.

Once you do get elected, learning how to, in humility, count others more significant than yourself becomes even more difficult. As I discussed earlier, as an elected official, you are usually treated special.

In *The Lord of the Rings* by J. R. R. Tolkien, there is one scene in which Frodo Baggins runs out to meet Gandalf as Gandalf arrives late in the Shire. Frodo exclaims, "Gandalf, you are late." Gandalf replies, "A wizard is never late, Frodo Baggins, nor is he early. He arrives precisely when he means to."[1]

The same is true for governors. If you are late, the state troopers who drive you everywhere can flip on their blue lights to go around the traffic jam. And since the governor is likely the focus of the event or meeting, even if you are late, the meeting is not going to start without you. There are multiple assistants to help schedule your days to maximize efficiency. You live in a Governor's Residence where someone else mows the lawn, cooks the meals, and cleans up after the events. And when you fly out of state, a state trooper from that state will meet you at the plane and whisk you off to wherever you are going. They probably have already checked you into your hotel room and even made sure your preferred snacks are in the room. It can all go to your head fairly quickly.

On one occasion, I was flying out of Nashville to the West Coast on Southwest Airlines. If you have ever flown on Southwest, you know the passengers can choose their seat in order of a boarding number received before the flight. Somehow, when you are governor, your number is always one. On this particular flight, I boarded the plane first and picked out my seat in the entirely empty plane. The next person to board was a woman who, having the whole rest of the plane to choose from, chose the seat right next to me. She proceeded to introduce herself and tell me how excited she was to be sitting next to the governor. I smiled, said thanks, and then she added, "for a four-hour flight!" *Oh boy*, I thought.

She then asked if she could take a selfie with me.

"Sure."

Then, as the plane slowly filled up with passengers, she asked, "Can we call my husband? He will think this is so cool."

"Why not," I replied.

After we finished talking to her husband, she asked, "Would it be okay if we FaceTime my office? They will not believe this."

As we ended the FaceTime with her office, a buzz spread over the now-almost-filled cabin of the plane. You could hear the sound of iPhone cameras clicking. I looked up to see the four lead singers of the award-winning country music group Little Big Town walking down the aisle to their seats.

Seeing them, my seatmate, who had been so excited to sit next to the governor, wrinkled her face and said, "Dang, now I don't feel like I got all that good of a seat."

Sometimes life itself has a way of reminding all of us, even governors, that we are not all that special.

While it sounds like I am writing only to those who run for office, I really believe these challenges come to anyone engaged in any way in the political process. Regardless of whether you are the candidate, a grassroots worker, a donor, or a vocal supporter, it is difficult to maintain a sense of godly humility. If we are honest, the more engaged we are, the more we want to win, so we can be proven right and score some points for our side. Humility that counts others more significant than ourselves quickly disappears, and we quickly forget that the purpose of the debate is for society to end up in a better place for the common good.

HUMILITY MEANS REMEMBERING WE HAVE NOT ALWAYS GOTTEN IT RIGHT

Peter was a product of a life of looking back and realizing how often he had not gotten it exactly right. Walking on water, only to sink when he noticed the wind. Cutting off the soldier's ear. Denying Jesus three times. The list goes on. All those events led the older, wiser, and humbler Peter to write, "Clothe yourselves, all of you, with humility toward one another, for 'God opposes the proud but gives grace to the humble'" (1 Peter 5:5).

Our humility, in politics and everywhere else, like Peter's, should spring from being forgiven and loved by the Creator of the universe. One of my favorite verses in the Bible occurs after Jesus' resurrection. Not yet having heard about the resurrection, most of the disciples were hiding in fear after Jesus' crucifixion, worried that they would be arrested for their association with him. Peter was not only fearful about that, but he was weighed down by the guilt of denying Jesus three times, just as Jesus predicted he would.

When Mary Magdalene; Mary, the mother of James; and Salome showed up at Jesus' tomb, they were planning to anoint the dead body. Seeing that the large rock guarding the tomb had been rolled away, they were alarmed to encounter an angel when they entered the tomb. The angel told the women not to be afraid and shared with them the world-changing news that Jesus of Nazareth was not there but was risen. Then he told them, "But go, tell his disciples *and Peter* that he is going before you to Galilee" (Mark 16:7, emphasis added). Don't you know that Peter was overjoyed with the reassurance that he was still included, despite what he had done? And don't you know that it was that forgiveness that led to his call to humility for us?

And if I am ever tempted to think I am indispensable to solving today's problems, I remind myself of the state capitol of Tennessee, where the portraits of former governors are placed in the main hall. There is a ceremony to unveil and hang the most recent governor's portrait prior to that governor leaving office. It is a nice honor, but a quick look around will tell you it is only temporary. There is room for only the most recent eight governors; the rest are taken to collect dust in a less prominent position. What an illustration of the fleeting nature of any recognition you get for power in the public square.

TRUTH WITH GRACE

The third area I have consistently found to be difficult to walk out as a Christian in politics regards a tension that I discussed earlier between justice and mercy, or truth and grace. Jesus was really clear when he said, "I am the way, and the truth, and the life" (John 14:6). Strong words. Paul also encouraged the Corinthians to be steadfast and immovable (1 Corinthians 15:58). There is no hint of mushiness here. There is no question that we are to be people of truth.

My concern is that, while Christians have become known for our commitment to truth, we have lost the ability to "[speak] the truth in love" (Ephesians 4:15). We have become dogmatic rather than following Paul's encouragement to let our reasonableness be known to everyone (Philippians 4:5). James expressed it this way: "The wisdom from above is first pure, then peaceable, gentle, open to reason, full of mercy and good fruits, impartial and sincere" (James 3:17).

Unfortunately, Christians in the public square are not known as peaceable or gentle, nor are we known for being open to reason. I am afraid that far more would describe us as strident than full of mercy. And I do not know about you, but I can rarely remember Christians encouraging one another to be impartial and sincere. We are so concerned with our passion for truth, we have forgotten how we are supposed to act as people of truth. How are we supposed to act? As people who are peaceable, gentle, open to reason, full of mercy and good fruits, and impartial and sincere.

Is it hard to be a Christian in politics? Yes. Not being anxious in a public role is only slightly less difficult than not being prideful. Turns out that being humble and unafraid in a public role requires truly trusting God. And, yes, it is difficult to be peaceable and gentle rather than firing back at those who disagree. I don't really want to be open to reason, impartial and sincere, when I am pretty sure I am right. And being full of mercy does not always feel as if it will straighten out the record in the way I think needs to happen.

Can these commands from Scripture actually work in these times of division and contempt?

7

DOES MEEKNESS HAVE A CHANCE?

I know many people will push back against the idea of being gentle and open to reason in politics. Their argument will be, "It's just not the way things work today. Nobody plays by Sunday school rules anymore. If we enter the political arena with a spirit of gentleness, being full of mercy and open to reason, we will get trounced by the other side. We are barely holding our own out there as it is right now."

It is a fair point. As I wrote earlier, the new world of social media and countless news options has produced fertile ground for the partisan politics of today. Candidates use negative advertising because it works, not because they enjoy being negative. Politics is a blood sport, the argument goes, and if you are going to win and be effective, you better not bring a pillow to a knife fight.

But does politics have to be a blood sport?

My first year in office as governor in 2011 was a time of political change in the country. President Obama had been elected in 2008, and his first midterm elections in 2010, like most midterm elections, saw a pendulum swing in the other direction. In this case, the pendulum swung back to the right, with Republicans winning twelve governor races that were previously held by Democrats, including mine. Many of my newly elected peers came out fighting and quickly established national reputations. One Tennessee commentator, lamenting the fact that I was not confrontational and loud enough for his taste, wrote me a letter saying, "These other states have superhero action figures for their new governor, and we are stuck with Mr. Rogers." I don't think he meant that as a compliment. Today's politics seems to require more than gentleness and being full of mercy. We cannot be expected to still play by the Sunday-school rules.

If we are tempted to think that today's political environment would be unrecognizable to the New Testament writers, it is worth remembering the Israel of Jesus' time. Like the Israel of today, it was a spiritual and political battleground. The Babylonians had destroyed the first temple five hundred years earlier. In 167 BC, the Syrians had taken over and desecrated the second temple. And, for the sixty years prior to Jesus' birth, the Roman Empire was in full control of Jerusalem. In addition, Israel had its own internal political parties. The Pharisees and Sadducees were only the best known out of scores of religious groups that were battling for supremacy.

Jesus' own birth had caused King Herod to murder every baby boy within Jesus' age range in an effort to eliminate this new future King. It was not a peaceful time, and the small band of early believers were not in a friendly environment. So it is not as if James, Jesus' brother, was unaware of how it feels to live in a heated, contentious culture when he instructed us to be gentle, full of mercy, and open to reason.

Personally, I would definitely have come up with a different strategy for winning the day in the political arena. My plan would have relied on hustle, muscle, and creative answers. But *gentle*, *full of mercy*, and *open to reason* are God's words. The same words that Timothy described as having been given to us so that the man of God may be "complete, equipped for every good work" (2 Timothy 3:17). *Equipped for every good work* seems like a pretty strong position to be in. My experience, after forty-five years of trying to follow God, is that doing things his way is more fruitful and productive than following my own strategy for success. As my friend and pastor Scott Sauls told me, "I have never met a follower of Christ who regretted obeying God. I have met a lot who regretted doing things their own way."

GOOD TO GREAT

In 2001, Jim Collins wrote the book *Good to Great,* and it almost instantly became a business classic. In the book, Collins sets out to discover what transforms businesses from good companies to great companies. In his words,

> We launched a six-month "death march of financial analysis," looking for companies that showed the following basic pattern: fifteen-year cumulative stock returns at or below the general stock market, punctuated by a transition point, then cumulative returns at least three times the market over the next fifteen years.[1]

In other words, these were companies that transformed from average performers to outstanding performers. They selected a period of fifteen years to make sure the company did not just get a lucky break. They also disqualified a company if their whole industry showed a similar increase.

The intent was to identify common characteristics of companies that met these criteria. From an initial study of 1,435 companies, only eleven were found to meet the standard. They also set out, without any preexisting answers, to discern what these companies might have in common. They were not trying to prove a theory, and they did not know what they would find.

What they discovered about the common characteristics of

the leaders of those great companies shocked them. As Collins put it, "Compared to high-profile leaders with big personalities who make headlines and become celebrities, the good-to-great leaders seem to have come from Mars. Self-effacing, quiet, reserved, even shy—these leaders are a paradoxical blend of personal humility and professional will. They are more like Lincoln and Socrates than Patton or Caesar."[2]

Is it surprising that a study of effective leadership would conclude that the very best leaders are those who lead like Jesus, even if they are not consciously doing so? Contrary to our fear of being rendered ineffective if we adapt a biblical approach to leading, the most effective leaders are those who realize that the best leadership comes from men or women who know that the story is not about them. Those leaders also know that the answers to the problems they are trying to solve are not about making a point; they are about making a difference.

CHANGING SOMEONE'S MIND

Our own life experience, along with Collins's research, tells us that the biblical approach truly is the most effective. Still, if you are like me, we think that our best hope of changing someone's mind is to passionately present our evidence of why *they* have gotten it wrong.

Have you ever really won an argument and changed someone's mind? Research shows that very few people change their mind because they lost an argument. In fact, if the argument contains insulting language, the effect is just the reverse. In 1967, researchers from Yale University published a study in the *Journal of Experimental Social Psychology* titled "Negative Persuasion via

Personal Insult." The article demonstrated what it referred to as the "boomerang effect," which is how, when you insult someone in an argument, they are three times more likely to harden their views and become more committed to their original position.[3]

If you still think the biblical approach will not work in elected office, think about Abraham Lincoln, the man generally considered our greatest president. His leadership strength grew out of his humility. It is hard to imagine many presidents who would write the words he wrote to General Ulysses S. Grant: "I now wish to make the personal acknowledgment that you were right, and I was wrong."[4] Or to admit, as Lincoln did to the troops of the 166th Ohio Regiment, "I happen temporarily to occupy this big white house. I am a living witness that any one of your children may look to come here as my father's child has."[5] That is the definition of meekness.

But all those in 1860 who mistook the new president's meekness for weakness were mistaken. This president was one who was strong enough to endure the death of over six hundred thousand people for America to remain undivided and for slavery to be abolished from our land. To put that in perspective, that is almost half of the total numbers of Americans who have died in all of our nation's wars. Anyone who can persist under the weight of losing so many, and withstand the criticism that came with it, is not someone who can be described as weak or timid. Meekness does not mean weakness.

WHY MEEKNESS WORKS

Right outside of the Sistine Chapel is a small room that has become known as the Crying Room. It is the room where the new pope, having just been elected by the College of Cardinals, first puts on the clothes of a pope. The name *Crying Room* comes from the story that the very best popes have been moved to tears at the responsibility before them as they prepared to meet the public for the first time as pope. Far from rejoicing over the new power they have been given, great leaders feel the weight of the responsibilities of the office and of their own inadequacy.

One of the most important things a governor does is propose the budget for the following year. The budget process is different in every state. Governors from other states have told me that their legislature typically ignored the governor's proposals and passed their own budget. In Tennessee, the legislature amends and adjusts the governor's budget, but most of what the governor proposes is passed and approved as the final budget. As with most families' household budgets, a state's budget always involves making difficult decisions about competing, worthy needs.

I still remember the weight our team felt in the early years of the administration. Because the budgets were tight, we had to eliminate some programs proposed by various departments. They were not bad programs; we just could not afford to do everything that was proposed. Still, it was sobering to make the decision that would mean not filling a need. It is, or should be, a humbling process to make decisions that will affect so many people's lives, but it is that humility and meekness that makes you especially equipped to do the job wisely and well.

Few people have shown the power of meekness in a political role like Nelson Mandela. For twenty-seven years he was held as a prisoner by his own government, a government that had come to embody racial injustice. He lost part of his sight from being unable to fend off the glare of the sun in the quarry where he worked all day breaking rocks. His cell was so small that he could barely lie down to sleep. If I were treated this unjustly, I would have a hard time responding to my captors with anything except bitterness and frustration. But Mandela thought it would be a character flaw to respond with anything other than kindness and respect. However, anyone who mistook his kindness and respect for an unwillingness to act against injustice was badly mistaken.

When he emerged from prison in 1990, he led the battle to end apartheid in South Africa. He was awarded the Nobel Peace Prize in 1993 for leading the effort for democratic change in a peaceful way. The next year he was elected president of South Africa, making the remarkable journey from prison to the presidency in four years. Arthur Brooks, in his book *Love Your Enemies*, wrote of Mandela:

> Deservedly, Mandela is remembered as one of history's greatest leaders. His greatness owes to his strength and courage, to be sure, but also to the goodness he displayed to everyone, including his captors. In modern life, we are taught that we have to choose between kindness and success; Mandela showed that this is not a choice we have to make. On the contrary, we can learn from this style of cheerful, kind leadership while striking a blow against the culture of contempt.[6]

It is tempting to think that the world has moved on from the humility of the postwar era and even from the 1990s of Nelson Mandela. Social media now provides the opportunity, or even the demand, for all of us to become our own publicist. Twitter, Instagram, and Facebook allow us to put together our own highlight reels. Politicians are no exception; in fact, we may be the leading example of how to promote oneself. The humble seem hopelessly ill-equipped for a world like this.

But it is worth remembering that the world of the New Testament seemed equally ill-suited for a message about the meek. Humility was definitely not a virtue in the Greek or Roman world. The Greek word for humility, *tapeinos*, was identified with failure, and it was never used in the context of approval, much less admiration. The meaning was closer to lowly or depressed.[7]

Instead of humility, Aristotle spoke of honor and reputation as goals worth seeking. Great leaders were supposed to be powerful and proud. That is why Jesus' death from crucifixion was so unexplainable in that culture. Crucifixion was not only the most brutal of the three official methods for execution (decapitation and being burned alive were the other choices), it was also the most shameful. How could the same Jesus who rode into Jerusalem to adoring crowds, who had established himself as a great teacher, end up on a cross, the worst place the culture of that day could envision?

Since the culture was all about avoiding shame, the clear implication was that not only was Jesus not the Messiah, he was also not even a great leader. No Roman emperor would have ever ended up on a cross. Today, two thousand years later, Christians see the crucifixion as evidence of the humility of Jesus, not a case of Jesus being humiliated.

Earlier I talked about the difficulty of being in the political world and living out Peter's call to "do nothing out of selfish ambition or vain conceit. Rather, in humility value others above yourselves" (Philippians 2:3 NIV). How in the world do we do that in today's political environment? Peter answers the question for all of us when he continues, "Have the same mindset as Christ Jesus: Who, being in very nature God . . . humbled himself by becoming obedient to death—even death on a cross" (Philippians 2:5–6, 8 NIV). As Christians, we follow someone who came not to kill the bad guys but to let the bad guys kill him.

Jesus is the most important figure in history. Peter and Paul would also be executed, both put to death by order of Nero. But their words and actions changed the way the world sees humility—and, in the process, changed the world.

Knowing that, the church today can and should be people who are known for entering the public square effectively with humility rather than pride and arrogance. It is simply the only way. Scripture doesn't come with exceptions for certain situations, like politics. But it does say that those who delight in the Lord will be "like a tree planted by streams of water that yields its fruit in its season, and its leaf does not wither" (Psalm 1:3).

8

CREATED IN THE IMAGE OF WHOM?

It was growing late on a Thursday night. I had been to several events that day and I was wrapping up the last thing on my schedule before a three-hour trip back to Nashville. As I got ready to head toward my car, a woman approached me and asked if she could have a quick word about something that was really upsetting her. I stopped and asked what was on her mind. She told me she was really upset that I had made our schools stop teaching cursive writing. She went on to explain that she had heard I had done that so kids would no longer be able to read the original copies of the Constitution and the Declaration of Independence. After I figured out that she was not joking and that she was convinced I had done this, I assured her what she had heard was not true. I had not taken cursive writing out of schools, and I actually wanted kids to know more about the founding documents of our country.

She wasn't buying my denial. She had read it on the internet from a very trusted source and had also heard it from a close friend. Our "quick word" was turning into a long conversation, and I was losing patience. Finally, I looked her in the eye one more time and promised her what she had heard was not true. She remained unconvinced as I climbed into the car.

This sort of thing happened frequently. I would find myself in a conversation with someone, or some group, and think, *How can they possibly think that way?* Or, on a less charitable day, *This person is crazy.* As a candidate or an officeholder, you meet a lot of people, and you have a lot of conversations. That is how democracy works. I was a lot better mayor and governor because I went through the process of campaigning. Stand on enough front porches and attend enough community meetings, and you learn what matters to people.

But talk to enough people and you will also run into some who leave you scratching your head, biting your tongue, or looking for the nearest exit. After one encounter with a man who was particularly challenging, I had finally freed myself and was walking back to the car when I heard one of our campaign aides whistling a tune. As I got closer to the car, I recognized it. It was a popular country music song at the time titled "People Are Crazy."

Are the people who disagree with us also created in the image of God? As absurd as the question is, I confess sometimes I have wondered.

MOVING PAST A CULTURE OF CONTEMPT

While we were in the Governor's Residence, Crissy and I developed a tradition of inviting legislators to dinner in small groups. Seated around the formal dining room, the guests had a chance to get to know one another on a more personal level. We had a standing rule that you could not use that time to lobby for a bill you favored or a position you held. I really enjoyed the conversations and the chance to get to know the legislators outside of the capitol. Yet, somehow, it inevitably seemed to happen that we'd invite someone who had recently very publicly criticized me or worked hard to stop one of our legislative initiatives. It occasionally felt like work to be the genial host.

All of us know the feeling of reading something or listening to someone and thinking that everything they are saying goes against what we believe to be true. And we can be assured that others feel the same way about us. How do we learn to make a distinction between people and their ideas? How do we learn to live with our deepest differences even when those differences push us to frustration?

If we are going to move past a culture of contempt, it is going to require humility and patience. Humility that recognizes we are not always right and patience to listen and understand.

This is another place where it is really hard to be someone who follows Jesus. We are called to love our enemies, not despise them, look down on them, ignore them, or even merely tolerate them. How do we do that?

When I find myself on the listening end of a long conversation with someone with different views, or when I read something from someone I disagree with, the first thing I have to remind myself is that this person is "created in the image of God." If I believe my friend, who thinks I am eliminating cursive writing so kids cannot read the Constitution and refused to accept my denial, really is created in the image of God, that changes everything. And if I believe my political opponent who has been attacking me every time he gets a chance is a fellow image bearer, my response has to reflect that reality.

C. S. Lewis described it this way: "It is a serious thing to live in a society of possible gods and goddesses . . . it is with the awe and the circumspection proper to them, that we should conduct all our dealings with one another, all friendships, all loves, all play, all politics."[1] If we believe we are who God says we are, then we have no choice but to look at those we disagree with in a different light. Lewis continued, "There are no ordinary people. You have never talked to a mere mortal . . . it is immortals whom we joke with, work with, marry, snub, and exploit."[2] And it is with this sober realization and acknowledgment of value that we must approach others, even and perhaps especially those we disagree with.

CREATED IN THE IMAGE OF GOD

The year 2020 was a painful year. The global pandemic caused by COVID-19 left hundreds of thousands dead, hospitalized many more, changed social habits, and created financial hardship as the economy was put into a self-induced coma. Unemployment soared to record highs, and the disparity in health conditions for people of color and low-income households was revealed to be even worse than feared. *Wall Street Journal* columnist Peggy Noonan, quoting writer Damian Barr, summed it up when she wrote, "We are not all in the same boat. We are all in the same storm."[3] And then, just as the United States was starting to come out of quarantine, we found ourselves in a world on fire with cries for justice after a black man was killed by a white police officer in Minneapolis. George Floyd's death, caused by an officer kneeling on his neck, was filmed and seen on television screens everywhere.

The African American community, and others, reacted out of the pain of generations of mistreatment. Protests spread across the country, many led by the Black Lives Matter (BLM) movement. Black Lives Matter's message was similar to the one on a poster Martin Luther King Jr. held when he marched in Memphis the day before he was assassinated: "I AM A MAN."

I can't help wondering, though, if perhaps BLM and Dr. King were aiming too low. Saying that black lives matter or asking for acknowledgment of one's humanity is only the first step in the call to recognize others as created in the image of God. White Christians should recognize not only that too many of us for too long have not treated people of color with respect, but that we also have not seen them as created in the image of God. Our racial problems are deep and long in this country, and we will not solve them overnight. But if we begin with the awareness that others are fellow image bearers, our discussions and interactions will change. This principle is applicable in all kinds of contexts.

Whatever policy decisions we are making, we must start with the core truth that all people are made in the image of God. When we don't, we move from disrespect to objectification, and eventually to the antithesis of seeing others as fellow image bearers, which is to see others as useful only for our purposes. When that idea gets carried out to its full conclusion, we see the tragedy of Nazi Germany. The death of roughly 6.5 million Jewish people is what happens when we ignore that people are created in the image of God. Another painful example is what the Nazis did to Russia.

Germany saw the vast Soviet Union as a potential grocery store. The fields and resources of the south were a "surplus" zone that produced food. Those who lived in the northern part of the country lived in the "deficit" zone and were seen as only consuming food that was produced in the south. The plan was to capture the surplus zone and divert its produce to Germany. The northern zone was to be cut off and ignored.[4]

The plan acknowledged that tens of millions of people in the Soviet Union would become superfluous and either starve to death or emigrate to Siberia, and any attempt to feed that population would just mean less food for Germany. Thus, they were expendable, and whatever happened to them was necessary for Germany to keep its people fed during the war.

Admittedly, the Holocaust and Nazis' willingness to starve millions of people are dramatic examples, and they might feel like a far cry from our tendency to see the folks on the other side of our politics as an enemy to be defeated. But this is the ultimate outcome of seeing others as either with us or against us, as less than fully created in the image of God.

THE IMAGE OF GOD IMPRINTED

The phrase *image of God* comes to us in the very first chapter of the Bible. In Genesis 1:26, God speaks to the other members of the Trinity and says, "Let us make man in our image." The author was so excited to communicate this truth that in the next verse he repeated himself on two occasions in the same verse: "So God created man in his own image, in the image of God he created him; male and female he created them" (v. 27).

Crissy's father was a heart surgeon. He was a pioneer in his field of cardiovascular surgery. Though he died in 1998, people still approach Crissy to tell her that her dad saved their life when he operated on them years ago. He also taught medical students and future surgeons at the University of Tennessee College of Medicine in Memphis.

We were at a campaign event in West Tennessee one night when a man came up to Crissy to ask if she was Ed Garrett's daughter. When she replied that she was, the man told Crissy he had done his surgical training under Dr. Garrett. Then he said, "To this day, when I am in the operating room, when I am in the middle of a difficult surgery, and I am not sure what to do, it is his voice I hear. I find myself holding my instruments the way he held his instruments and trying to do surgery the way he did surgery."

In the process of teaching medical students how to repair hearts, my father-in-law had passed on not only his surgical knowledge but enough of himself that forty years later his image was still imprinted on his former students. Because of that, there are numerous heart surgeons who operate like Ed Garrett. It's the same with us and God.

It is a mystery to me why God imprinted his image on us. It is hard enough for me to see myself that way, and even harder for me to see people I disagree with that way. Yet I am convinced that if we are going to heal the division in our country, this is the foundational truth that can bridge the gap most of us despair of ever bridging.

Our political divide seems to be not only growing but growing more bitter. That divide would surely narrow if we recognized Lewis's point that even those who frustrate us because they see the world so differently than we do are not "ordinary people" and that we have never met a "mere mortal." If that commentator on the news channel who makes me so mad is created in the image of God, I have to see him or her in a different way. And if my neighbor who always has a yard sign up for the wrong candidate really does bear the image of God, I cannot pull into my driveway every evening wishing for a different neighbor. Lewis continued in *The Weight of Glory*, "Next to the Blessed Sacrament itself, your neighbor is the holiest object presented to your senses."[5]

Whether it is one of my children, my wife, a staff member, or a legislator, I am better to them when I realize the truth that they are not only children of their parents but also—and more importantly—children of God. I am kinder, more thoughtful, more patient, and more open.

I have also found that when I understand the person in front of me is a child of God and treat them as such, they are more open to me. They are more open to my ideas, just as I am to theirs. The world not only needs Christians to lead with proper ideology; it needs Christians to lead in their understanding that, at our root, we are deeply connected. We are all made in the image of God.

And so, whatever our disagreements may be, we can take a page from Martin Luther King Jr.'s book about this idea of the image of God being the foundation for progress, as elusive as it may be. In his sermon titled "The American Dream," King said,

> You see, the founding fathers were really influenced by the Bible. The whole concept of the *imago dei*, as it is expressed in Latin, the "image of God," is the idea that all men have something within them that God injected. Not that they have substantial unity with God, but that every man has a capacity to have fellowship with God. And this gives him a uniqueness, it gives him worth, it gives him dignity. And we must never forget this as a nation: there are no gradations in the image of God. Every man from a treble white to a bass black is significant on God's keyboard, precisely because every man is made in the image of God.[6]

—— 9 ——

WHAT ABOUT THE SEPARATION OF CHURCH AND STATE?

I was visiting a farmers market in a rural part of our state as part of an agriculture promotion highlighting Tennessee-grown products. I had spent the better part of a week visiting farms all over the state so I could learn more about agriculture as well as promote Tennessee farms. Crissy had reminded me not to come home empty-handed, so I saved some time to shop for fresh fruits and vegetables.

As I worked my way through the crowd, I noticed an elderly gentleman who had been waiting his turn to talk to me. When we did get a chance to talk, he struck me as a kind and gentle man, so, unlike in some situations, I was not too worried when he said, "I want to ask you a question." But I was a little surprised when he asked, "So, why did you veto the Bible?"

Earlier that year, our legislature had passed a bill making the Bible Tennessee's official state book. Tennessee, like most states, has a number of official state items, ranging from the state insect (ladybug) to the state flower (iris). Thus, the newly passed bill would recognize the Bible as our official state book.

I vetoed only five bills during the entire eight years I was in office. How could a professing Christian veto making the Bible our official book? The bill sponsors felt strongly that this was one way to fight back against the secular tide and put a stake in the ground. As you can imagine, the bill's opponents raised loud complaints about the separation of church and state. Some people argued that it was not a big deal one way or the other. After all, even as governor, I could not have passed a test that asked me to name the state drink (milk, but I would have guessed Jack Daniel's) or the state song (trick question—there are nine others besides "Rocky Top"). But the question the elderly gentleman asked me at the farmers market was a good one. To understand the answer, we need to talk about what the separation of church and state means—and does not mean.

This topic has caused fundamental disagreements for our entire history as a country. We live in a pluralistic society. There is not one ultimate source of authority as a country, and even the Supreme Court has not painted clear lines. Because of this, all of us, and especially any Christian leader, should use wisdom to think deeply about these complicated issues.

At times, in office, we have to make decisions that seem counter to our beliefs. When that happens, it is easy to assume that the decision is being made for political reasons. While sometimes that might be a correct assumption, often there are reasons that involve the long-term consequences of the decision or a dangerous precedent that it might set. The "Bible bill," as it became known, was one of those cases.

The prior year, our attorney general had opined that designating the Bible as the official state book would violate the establishment clause of the First Amendment to the federal Constitution and the Tennessee Constitution. The First Amendment provides that no preference should ever be given, by law, to any religious establishment or mode of worship. The sponsors of the bill had attempted to avoid that issue by saying they were recognizing the Bible not as a religious book but as one with historic and economic significance.

Beyond the constitutional issues, I had personal concerns. As I wrote in my veto letter to the speakers of our Tennessee house and senate:

In addition to the constitutional issues with the bill, my personal feeling is that this bill trivializes the Bible, which I believe is a sacred text. If we believe that the Bible is the inspired Word of God, then we shouldn't be recognizing it only as a book of historical and economic significance. If we are recognizing the Bible as a sacred text, then we are violating the Constitution of the United States and the Constitution of the State of Tennessee by designating it as the official state book. Our founders recognized that when the church and state were combined, it was the church that suffered in the long run.[1]

Our struggle over the relationship between religion and government is not new. In fact, the struggle precedes our country even being a country. Around 140 years before the Declaration of Independence, the Massachusetts Bay Colony consisted of men and women who had fled Europe in order to enjoy religious freedom to worship as they pleased. Two of their leaders, John Winthrop and Roger Williams, disagreed over how much the church should control the state. Winthrop was the composer of the vision for this new country to be a "city upon a hill,"[2] dedicated to God's laws and serving as a model for the rest of the world to observe. Williams, on the other hand, argued that the state forcing religion on its citizens "stinks in God's nostrils."[3] Winthrop recognized Williams as a godly minister, and they both believed that their purpose was to advance the kingdom of God. But their differing visions resulted in Williams being thrown out of the Massachusetts Bay Colony and going on to plant the city of Providence and what became the state of Rhode Island.

Arguments today about prayer in schools or having the Ten Commandments on courthouse walls are only the latest iterations of a centuries-old debate. America's early settlers from Europe struggled with the same issue, and the founders of our country wrestled with the same questions. They knew and remembered the religious persecution that caused their grandparents and great-grandparents to come to this country. Because of that, they wanted to establish a limited government that could not force its faith on anyone. The result was the First Amendment. It says, "Congress shall make no law respecting an establishment of religion, or prohibiting the free exercise thereof; or abridging the freedom of speech, or of the press; or the right of the people peaceably to assemble, and to petition the government for a redress of grievances."

It is important to note that there are two clauses in the First Amendment related to religion. One of the clauses prohibits the establishment of a government-sponsored religion. There would be no state church in America. The other clause, equally important, prevents the prohibition of the free exercise of religion.

The inclusion of both of those points was groundbreaking. As Senator Ben Sasse says in his book *Them*, "Before Philadelphia in 1787, most people assumed that government needed to define true religion. Across most of Europe, religious and cultural unity was enforced by the state."[4] One of the key reasons so many people fled Europe for America was that religious dissent from the official state church was not allowed. Sasse continues, "The framers' view, our view, is different: we begin by announcing that religion is so important that the central government doesn't get to be in the business of religion at all."[5] The government could not be used to establish one religion over another. And, just as importantly, it could not be used to stop the free practice of religion.

The founders obviously wrestled with how to set the right relationship between the church and state. They knew they did not want a state religion, but they also knew the form of government they were establishing assumed a flourishing religious environment. John Adams, though not particularly devout himself, spoke to that tension:

> We have no government armed with power capable of contending with human passions unbridled by morality and religion. Avarice, ambition, revenge or gallantry, would break the strongest cords of our Constitution as a whale goes through a net. Our Constitution was made only for a moral and religious people. It is wholly inadequate to the government of any other.[6]

I think the founders got it right when it came to the relationship between religion and government. Again, when the church and state are combined, it is usually the church that loses. For proof, look no further than Europe. The state-sanctioned religion that chased so many of our ancestors out of Europe to America has resulted in a European continent where it is hard to find many signs of life in the church. Despite all the continent's beautiful cathedrals, the church has struggled to stay alive, and Europe is a largely secular land today.

The balancing act the founders sought is one of the most unique features of our remarkable form of government. As Peter Wehner says in *The Death of Politics*, "America's combination of the separation between religion and politics, alongside its protection of religious minorities, has made it the exception among developing nations: a flourishing religious culture in which no one sect serves as the established faith for the nation."[7]

While I have primarily focused on the benefits of not having a state-sponsored church, I deeply believe that the second religious clause of the First Amendment has been just as important for the flourishing of the United States. It is not just that Congress could make no law establishing religion; they also could not make law that prohibited the free exercise of that religion. The government was not to prevent people from worshipping the way they wanted.

The beauty of the idea of America is that we can all bring our most deeply held beliefs to the public square, without the government declaring one faith or no faith the winner—and without any faith or person of faith being excluded from the debate. I would argue that it is this truth that led people of faith, like Abraham Lincoln and Martin Luther King Jr., to push the country toward living out in practice what the founders declared on paper when they wrote that "all men are created equal [and] endowed by their Creator with certain unalienable rights."

Today, the debate about religion and government often plays out around the contentious issues of human sexuality. Many commentators have pointed out a growing political divide between rural and urban areas, college graduates and noncollege graduates, and older and younger voters. But perhaps the sharpest debates, and the sharpest political divides, have been around issues of abortion and gay marriage. Once again, the issue of religious liberty is at the forefront of the debate. Does religious expression still have a place in the public square?

Two cases gained a lot of attention on the national scene. The first involved the Obama administration suing the Little Sisters of the Poor. The Little Sisters of the Poor are an order of nuns with a mission to serve the elderly and the poor. They had refused to follow a mandate from the US Department of Health and Human Services (HHS) to provide an insurance plan covering abortifacient drugs and contraceptives. HHS had given them a narrow exemption, saying this would not apply to any religious employer who did not serve people outside of their own faith. Obviously, the sisters and most other faith-based groups exist to serve people inside and outside of their own faith. They cannot carry out their mission if they serve only those inside their faith, and they would not want to serve only in that way. Beyond the horrible optics of suing a group called the Little Sisters of the Poor, many Americans felt this was another case of a heavy-handed government working to force religious believers away from the free exercise of their religion.

The other case involved a Colorado baker, Jack Phillips, and his Masterpiece Cakeshop. In 2012, Phillips refused to make a cake for a same-sex wedding ceremony. He told the couple he would be glad to make them a birthday cake or serve them anything else, but he could not make a cake to promote their same-sex marriage due to his religious beliefs. The ACLU represented the same-sex couple in their complaint against Phillips. The Colorado Office of Administrative Courts ruled that the bakeshop had violated a Colorado statute that said businesses could not refuse service based on a potential customer's sexual orientation. After losing their appeal, Masterpiece Cakeshop was ordered to change its policies and provide comprehensive staff training to all its employees.

The Colorado Supreme Court refused to hear the case after the Colorado Court of Appeals ruled that Phillips's religious beliefs were not a valid reason to refuse service to the same-sex couple. In June 2017, almost five years after the couple had visited Masterpiece Cakeshop looking for a wedding cake, the US Supreme Court agreed to hear the case. One year later, it ruled 7 to 2 in favor of Phillips and Masterpiece Cakeshop. The Court said, "While it is unexceptional that Colorado law can protect gay persons in acquiring products and services on the same terms and conditions as are offered to other members of the public, the law must be applied in a manner that is neutral toward religion."[8]

Justice Anthony Kennedy, frequently a swing vote on the Court during his time on the bench, said that when the Colorado Civil Rights Commission made its decision, it did not do so "with the religious neutrality that the Constitution requires." The opinion says the commission "violated the Free Exercise Clause; and its order must be set aside."[9] As you can see, though Christians often see the separation of church and state as a barrier, it is actually more complex than most realize. It can be a real help to those looking to practice their faith without government interference.

UNPOPULAR DECISIONS

When I was elected governor, countless people told me how happy they were that we had a Christian governor. While I usually just politely thanked them, I always wanted to ask, What do you mean by that? Just what are you expecting a Christian governor to do? For some, it meant we would now have a big push to return prayer to schools. Others hoped I would hire only Christians for important positions, particularly judges. And many would say that they wanted someone who was going to stop the cultural decline and make Tennessee the shining city upon a hill, the goal of the Christians who left Europe to settle in New England in 1620.

Many of the people who were excited to have a new Christian governor inaugurated in 2011 were disappointed by a decision I made in the spring of 2012. Vanderbilt University had adopted an all-comers policy, which meant that "All students are presumed to be eligible for membership in registered student organizations

(RSO) and all members of RSOs in good standing are eligible to compete for leadership positions."[10] This meant that under Vanderbilt's nondiscrimination policy, to remain on campus a student group could not exclude anyone from membership or from holding a leadership position in the organization. Although the university's nondiscrimination policy had been in place for a long time, Vanderbilt did not begin enforcing it until 2012.

Vanderbilt's policy meant that college Republicans would have to allow Democrats to join and vice versa, and that Muslim students could join Hillel and atheists could join religious groups. Most student organizations said they were fine with that part of the policy and even welcomed the opportunity to share their views with others. The part of the policy that caused the most disagreement was requiring all group members to be eligible for leadership positions.

Our legislature reacted to Vanderbilt's new enforcement of the policy by passing a bill that prohibited an all-comers policy at our state's public colleges and universities. However, because Vanderbilt is a private institution, they would not be impacted by the new law. The legislature then passed a bill prohibiting an all-comers policy at any institution that received more than $24 million a year from the state. Vanderbilt received that much money in state funding through Medicaid dollars that went to its hospital, which at the time was a part of the university. If I signed the bill, and it became law, Vanderbilt would either have to change its policy or lose Medicaid funding for its hospital patients.

To be clear, I disagreed with Vanderbilt's policy. It is important to note that all the student groups that disagreed with the policy had no issue with making their membership open to all students. But they did think it was important that they have leaders who agree with their core beliefs. I think most Americans would concur that it is reasonable for groups to be able to select leaders based on that group's beliefs and practices. The surface issue that drew most of the attention was around some of the campus religious groups and questions of sexuality.

I thought then, as I do now, that the bigger issue was whether groups with different beliefs could coexist on a campus. The question was about what the much-praised virtue of tolerance looks like. Vanderbilt's actions felt like an admission that navigating the waters of pluralism in a university setting is not just difficult but impossible. It is the same mentality NYU professor Tamarie Macon identified when one of her students said, "We can only discuss when we all agree."[11] The university setting that was once the premier marketplace of ideas seems to struggle now with tolerating conflicting moral and religious ideas.

The bill prohibiting an all-comers policy at any institution that received any state funds was passed by the legislature by an overwhelming margin in the house and the senate. I immediately started getting calls from the leaders of many of the national Christian ministries with chapters on the Vanderbilt campus, urging me not to veto the bill. Several of the calls were from people I knew and respected. They stressed that the issue was much larger than Vanderbilt. A few other schools had adopted similar policies, and many more schools were considering it and following this case closely. I understood why this was a big issue for the leaders of these ministries, and I shared many of their concerns.

However, I had other issues to consider. The primary one was this: Should the state tell a private institution like Vanderbilt how it should conduct its business? It is one thing for the state to decide the policies of our own public institutions, but it felt like an entirely different thing for the state to determine policies for a private university. This time it was a conservative legislature rebuking Vanderbilt. But in another time it might be, and in some places already is, a legislature telling a Christian college what it can or cannot do.

Thus, my very first veto—one of only five that I issued—was to stop a bill that was trying to address something I agreed was a problem. The reality is that politicians, even Christians in politics, sometimes have to make decisions that seem counter to our personal beliefs. It does not always signify mushiness or flip-flopping. It could be the reality of governing in a pluralistic setting and being cognizant of constitutional limits and dangers precedents can set, like the state telling a private institution what it can and cannot do.

While the decisions I made on the Bible bill and the Vanderbilt all-comers bill left many on the right disappointed in me, a decision I made in 2016 resulted in people on the left being upset with me. Senate Bill 1556, known as the "counseling bill," said that no licensed counselor or therapist had to serve a client whose goals, outcomes, or behaviors conflicted with the counselor's sincerely held principles. The bill would also protect counselors from civil lawsuits, criminal prosecution, and sanctions by the state for refusing to provide services.

There were two key provisions to the bill. First, before denying service, a counselor had to coordinate the referral of the client to another counselor who would serve them. Second, the bill would not apply to any situation in which the person seeking counseling was in imminent danger of harming themselves or others.

The bill stemmed from a 2014 change the American Counseling Association (ACA) made to its code of ethics. The

ACA had made the change to protect counseling clients from discrimination. This became a state issue because the state's licensing board for professional counselors and marital and family therapists uses the ACA's code of ethics for its rules and regulations. So, if a counselor violated the ACA's code of ethics, he or she would then be subject to sanction by the state.

The bill passed the senate by a 27 to 5 margin and was approved by the house with a vote of 68 to 22. Immediately, we began to receive a lot of pressure from the ACA, the ACLU, and others to veto the bill. And because it was a "religious freedom" issue, it quickly attracted a lot of national attention. Despite the bill's requirement that counselors coordinate referral to another provider, and that treatment cannot be refused to anyone perceived to be in imminent danger, the national headlines made it sound as if it were a license for counselors to deny treatment to gay people at their lowest points.

There was also concern that the headlines would chase away conventions and businesses. North Carolina's recently passed "bathroom bill," which required transgender people to use bathrooms that corresponded with the gender on their birth certificate in government and public buildings, had generated a lot of national attention and threats from businesses to relocate away from North Carolina. The NBA had canceled an All-Star basketball game scheduled for Charlotte. Similarly, the ACA and a couple of other small organizations canceled conventions scheduled for Nashville due to our counseling bill.

I spent a lot of time talking with counselors who were for and against the bill. My job was to look at the actual substance of the bill, not just the media reports and emails sent to our office. We already allowed other professionals, like doctors and lawyers, to refer clients to another provider when the goals of their service violated a sincerely held belief. In the same way, no person seeking counseling would be turned away without access to another provider.

My decision to sign the bill was met with a predictable chorus of disapproval from those who saw the bill as another form of discrimination. Harvard's School of Education withdrew an offer for me to speak, and several newspapers editorialized their disagreement.

To me this bill was another case of making certain that we did not violate the free exercise clause of the Constitution. Many of the counselors I talked with who were in favor of the bill said they currently counsel gay clients who need therapy on a wide range of issues, just as they do straight clients. However, when a client came to them with a value conflict, genuine service for the client would mean referring them to someone who did not have that conflicting value. For many Christian counselors, this would mean their inability to provide sex therapy to an unmarried couple as well as a same-sex couple.

WISDOM OF THE FOUNDERS

The wisdom of our founders in including the establishment clause and the free exercise of religion clause in the First Amendment can be found in the Bible bill, the all-comers bill, and the counseling bill. Our government is one that does not establish any religion as the policy of the state. It also is one that is supposed to do nothing to prohibit the free exercise of its citizens' faith. Given that, what should it mean to be a Christian governor? Or a Christian mayor, president, school board member, or any other elected office?

As we have seen, it should not mean that we establish our faith as the country's or state's or city's faith. The Constitution prohibits it, and we know from experience that doing so does not end well for the church. It is hard to think of an example anywhere or from any time in history where the state-established church has led to a healthy and flourishing church. The church has been much more likely to grow and thrive under difficult conditions.

The second thing that being a Christian in public life should not mean is that we discriminate or be hostile toward other faiths. The freedom of exercise clause applies to other faiths just as much as it does to our own. As John Inazu, Constitutional scholar from Washington University, says, our call is to be "respectful even when we disagree."[12] He also points out that "tolerance isn't indifference."[13] This means that we are not indifferent and without opinions about the truth claims of other religions and worldviews. We are not surrendering our view of truth, or even the idea that there is a truth. We can recognize the constitutional rights of other faiths and respect their rights to worship as they choose without affirming all their doctrine.

Anti-Muslim feelings were particularly strong during my time in office. Coming on the heels of 9/11 and with the country's ongoing wars in Iraq and Afghanistan, a fear of "Sharia law" was gaining a foothold in America. This concern led to a couple of humorous events and some that were not so funny.

One time I was dining with a local pastor and a friend of his who had been a pastor in Iraq. We were having lunch in the Capitol Grille, a restaurant right across the street from the state capitol. The restaurant was always full of legislators and other officials due to its proximity to state offices. Before we ate, I asked the visiting pastor if he would say a blessing for our meal. He readily agreed and then asked if it was okay with us if he prayed in Jesus' language, Arabic. He then began to pray. In Arabic. Very loudly. Loud enough to get the attention of everyone in the room. Loud enough to cause more than a few of the diners to suspect that the governor was having a Muslim prayer meeting in the Capitol Grille.

That same year, we were doing some maintenance and renovation on the state's historic capitol building. Originally finished in 1859, the building looks much the same as it did when it was completed, and it is one of the oldest-working capitols in the United States. There was never a day when I did not think it was a special privilege to work in this beautiful building. However, as you can imagine, like any other 150-year-old building, it needed some maintenance and work at times. So, in 2012, we moved our offices out of the capitol while the plumbing, electrical, and mechanical systems were upgraded. One of the upgrades was adding a floor-level sink for housekeeping purposes. This sparked rumors and concerns from some of our legislators that the sink was for Muslims to wash their feet before praying. The true purpose of housekeeping caused the *Chattanooga Times Free Press* to write, "Sometimes a mop sink is just a mop sink."[14]

It was a little less humorous when radio talk show hosts and others attacked a member of our administration because she was Muslim. Although she grew up in a small town in Tennessee, her father had served as president of the Tennessee Medical Association and as an officer in the Tennessee National Guard, and she had been a White House Fellow, unfair and untrue accusations were made that she had connections to terrorists and the Muslim Brotherhood. She worked in our Department of Economic & Community Development as an assistant commissioner, and her job was to promote international trade with

Tennessee, not Sharia finance. She was there to serve Tennessee, not infiltrate the government as anonymous critics alleged. Our job in leading a government is to make sure we hire the best team of people to serve the citizens of the state, not the people who have the same religious beliefs that we do. If I were going in for brain surgery, I would be much more focused on the surgeon's training than on where he or she worships.

That being said, I would never have run for mayor or governor if not for my Christian faith. For me, the call to public service was just that: a call. My reason for being in the public square was my desire to be faithful to what I thought God was leading me to do. While I enjoyed my business career, no job ever felt as much like a calling, like what I was meant to do, as serving in office.

The idea that religious people should not bring their deepest desires and commitments to public debate is not constitutional or historic. Ours is a country that was begun by people seeking religious freedom, and the Declaration of Independence and the Constitution are infused with the idea of religion as a motivating factor for the birth of the country. It is not realistic that we should act without personal conviction.

All of us bring our worldviews as a beginning point, religious or not, to the public arena. We are all served best by people who are not running for office for their own personal reward. Our best public servants are those who are there to serve. Christians should understand this concept because that is what we are called to do, regardless of where we are called. We are the ones who should be trying to follow Jesus and his reminder that even "the Son of Man came not to be served but to serve" (Matthew 20:28).

This reminder applies even, or maybe especially, in the public square.

10

CYNTOIA AND THE BEAUTY OF THE GOSPEL

Our struggle, in public life and everywhere else, is to know how to be just and merciful at the same time.

After almost eight years of serving as the governor of Tennessee, my staff and I were accustomed to getting a lot of feedback. Emails, phone calls, Tweets, Facebook posts, letters, and office visits are part of the currency of modern democracy, and we learned that people are rarely shy about expressing their opinions.

So, with only a couple of months left in my time as Tennessee's governor, I was surprised to see my assistant and the front office receptionist walk into my office with alarm written all over their faces. Both of them had been around the entire time we had been in office, so they had seen a lot.

"We have never seen anything like this before," they said. Our phone system was overwhelmed, and constituent services could not keep up with all the emails and letters. "This Cyntoia Brown deal is out of control."

Cyntoia Brown had been convicted as a sixteen-year-old in August 2004 for the murder of Johnny Michael Allen. Tragically, like many other teenage girls, she had been caught up in the horrible world of sex trafficking. After being paid $150, she agreed to go home with Allen, a man who had solicited her for sex. Later that night, Cyntoia shot Allen and killed him. She said she shot him because she feared for her life. Prosecutors said she shot him in the back of the head, robbed him, and stole his truck. Tried as an adult, she was sentenced to life in prison. Her first chance for parole would be in fifty-one years when she was sixty-seven years old.

Cyntoia, whose early teenage years had been a picture of heartbreak, matured into a woman intent on living a different life, a life that spoke of a God who is relentless in helping us experience mercy, grace, and transformation. While in prison, she became a voice for repentance, justice, and freedom. She earned her bachelor's degree with a 4.0 GPA from Lipscomb University. And, as I prepared to leave the governor's office in early 2019, she still had more than thirty-six years left on her sentence.

Her situation came to national attention with the documentary *Me Facing Life: Cyntoia's Story*. It gained a lot more notice when her cause was taken up by a slew of celebrities. As a governor, you have something of a bully pulpit. If you call a news conference, the newspapers and television stations will usually cover what you have to say, and you have frequent opportunities to speak around the state and country. However, all that pales in comparison to the reach of a celebrity with a huge social media following. Today's entertainment and athletic celebrities have millions of followers on their social media, and those followers quickly react to any call for action.

So, when Kim Kardashian, Rihanna, Snoop Dogg, and Lebron James sent out tweets with #freeCyntoia, it got a lot of response. Cyntoia's cause was taken up by advocates against human trafficking as well as groups working for sentencing reform and against racism. It brought together an unlikely coalition of white evangelicals, BLM advocates, and others who were moved by her story.

As I was thinking through the hundreds of other requests for pardons and commutations, public pressure for Cyntoia continued to grow. Much of it was thoughtful. Much of it aligned with my administration's desire to stop human trafficking. And the case brought long-overdue attention to the ongoing tragedy of sex trafficking. Cyntoia was a teenage girl under the control of a pimp, who acted like he was her boyfriend. No teenage girl chooses to be a prostitute.

Cyntoia's situation also highlighted the injustice of a sixteen-year-old being given a life sentence and ineligible for parole until she was sixty-seven. Others rightly pointed out the racial disparities of our incarceration rates. Black and white; liberal and conservative; Christian, Jew, and Muslim—something about Cyntoia's case touched people of all persuasions.

Others were not as thoughtful. Some state legislators decided it would be better to call a press conference to demand that I free Cyntoia, even though they could have come and asked me personally anytime they wanted.

One night in early December, I was part of an education forum at the Nashville Public Library with the opinion editor of the *Tennessean*, the Nashville daily newspaper. Shortly after the event began, a group with bullhorns took over and demanded I make a commitment to free Cyntoia right then or else they would continue to disrupt the event and any other events I attended. After patiently listening to them and explaining why I would not make such a commitment that night, the group continued to make their demand with bullhorns. Finally, we had no choice but to cancel the remainder of the forum.

Deciding whether to intervene in the judicial process with the power of the office of the governor is rarely a clear and obvious choice. But I do know for certain that a decision like this should not be made by the number of emails, Tweets, and phone calls I receive. When you think about it, nobody, even Cyntoia's biggest supporters, should want that to be the reason we decided to commute her sentence. That would be similar to making a decision based on what your campaign donors wanted or what your political adviser said would be the best for your political future. A decision about clemency should be made on the merits of the case, not the politics that come out of it.

To her credit, Cyntoia understood her situation to be one of justice, not of politics, as well as anyone. When I talked with her later, she said she always had a sinking feeling in her stomach when she heard about some of the ways people expressed their thoughts on her release. Her fear was that would make us less likely to release her. I continuously wrestled to make sure we did not treat her case any easier or harder because of all the attention it was getting. I was not sure of the right thing to do in this case, but I knew that justice would not be served by a decision based on how I felt about the ways people were pleading her case.

Another thing made this case difficult. In the process of researching Cyntoia's case, I became aware that more than 180 others were in prison and sentenced to life as juveniles. At this point, I did not have time to research every one of those cases. But it was safe to assume that many of them had arguments just as compelling as Cyntoia's. They just had not benefited from all the publicity. Was it fair to single her out when others could possibly have as good of a case but without the national spotlight?

There were many other factors for me to consider. On the one hand, a murder was committed that even Cyntoia described as horrific. On the other hand, there was her background and the adverse childhood experiences that led her to being on the streets by the time she was thirteen. There was also the reality that Cyntoia was a victim of sex trafficking. And, again, no teenage girl chooses to be a prostitute.

As you can imagine, our legal team and I wrestled hard with all of this. We were struggling with how to be just and merciful at the same time.

There is a small kitchen area just off the governor's conference room in the capitol. Hanging on the wall, above my not-so-secret stash of candy and crackers, were the framed words of Micah 6:8: "He has told you, O man, what is good; and what does the LORD require of you but to do justice, and to love kindness, and to walk humbly with your God?"

How does that work? How do we do justice and love mercy at the same time? Everyone wants their leaders to be loving and merciful. Beyond that, we know we are all called, elected officials or not, to be people of justice and mercy. We are drawn to a God whose "mercies never come to an end; they are new every morning" (Lamentations 3:22–23). We know we need a God who is merciful when it comes to our sinfulness and shortcomings. Yet, as a society, we demand justice.

I gained a fresh appreciation for the beauty of the gospel while I wrestled through all the decisions around pardons and commuting sentences that were before me, struggling with how to be just and merciful at the same time. The story of Jesus coming to live and die is the story of a God of justice who knew we needed mercy. His justice demanded that a price be paid for our rebellion against him. His mercy was not without cost. His mercy meant that, in the greatest love story ever told, it was his own Son who had to be sacrificed.

The only biblical way for us to walk into the public square is the way Jesus walked toward the cross. His motivation was his love for a broken and hurting people. It was not to be proven right or to win the argument or to gain power for himself.

Too often, I see people who are in the public square solely

to win the argument. My experience is that Christians are as guilty of that as everyone else. Our motivation for walking into the public square should always reflect our call to serve, not our desire to win. As said in Scripture, "But the wisdom from above is first pure, then peaceable, gentle, open to reason, full of mercy and good fruits, impartial and sincere. And a harvest of righteousness is sown in peace by those who make peace" (James 3:17–18).

The One who has granted us mercy with justice is asking us to do justice and love mercy. We are in public life because, out of response to his great love for us, we want to bring healing to a broken world. Scripture seems pretty clear on how we are to do that, and it is worth repeating: do it with the wisdom that is pure, peaceable, gentle, reasonable, merciful, impartial, and sincere.

That kind of wisdom might not lead to a lot of likes on your Facebook page. It is easily drowned out by the shouting voices on cable TV. It might not even feel as good as finally being able to unload our opinions we think the world so desperately needs to hear. But it does lead to a harvest of righteousness. I am not much of a farmer, so I do not have a lot of mental pictures of bringing in the harvest. But I can appreciate the beautiful image of reaping barns full of righteousness as God's provision for us and his blessing for others.

A GOVERNOR'S ABSOLUTE POWER

Some people confuse being a governor with being a king and think that the governor can make happen whatever he or she desires. These folks obviously have never met a state legislature! For good reasons, the governor's power has checks and balances.

That is our democratic system, and it often moves slowly, if it moves at all.

One area where the governor's power is almost absolute, though, is the power to grant pardons and clemency and to commute sentences. The president and most governors have the power to intervene in the judicial system so there is someone who can step in when something needs to be addressed that the court system cannot. I think that ability has been a useful backstop in a lot of cases. But like any other power, it can be abused. The governor can empty the state's prisons in a matter of hours if he or she desires, unless it is in exchange for financial reward. One of my predecessors in Tennessee tried that and ended up spending some time in one of those same prisons.

Early in my time in office, I made the decision to delay all requests for pardons, clemencies, and commutations until my last months in office. Several former governors had advised me that I did not want to have people approaching me throughout my time in office with requests to consider their legal situation.

You might be amazed to learn how many people you know who have something in their past they would like to clean up. Perhaps it was a DUI, a conviction for selling marijuana, or any number of things. Additionally, there are even more folks whom the governor will never meet but who are eager to submit requests for some type of judicial relief. For many of them, the governor is the only hope for adjusting their sentence in the foreseeable future.

At the time, I thought it would be best to listen to the advice I had received and wait to review these requests. I did not want to be preoccupied with this throughout the entire eight years in office. I thought it would be better to delay all those decisions until the end and deal with them all at the same time.

In hindsight, this was a bad decision. Really bad.

In my mind, I thought that with the assistance of my legal team I could figure out a way, case by case, to be both just and merciful. I thought it would be easy to be fair and show grace at the same time. Our team could work to understand the situation behind each offense and each offender, and we could weigh the impact of the crime on the victims, their families, and their communities. We could also evaluate the difference a pardon or commutation might make in the applicant's future life. And, of course, you could clearly judge what the offender's life had been like since the offense. After all that, we could then make a decision that would balance justice and mercy, or so I thought, before I began working my way through the requests.

While few of us have the power to grant clemency, we have all had to decide whether or not to fire somebody, promote somebody, or especially, to forgive somebody of a wrong they have done to us or our organization. In a way, we have all had to weigh the balance between mercy and justice more frequently than we would like. But, while I had wrestled with the choice between justice and mercy before, it was a lot harder than I thought to do it on a public stage.

Having been granted this power by the Constitution of the state of Tennessee, it was clearly my responsibility to use it wisely and never to abuse it in any way. As much as your heart wants to be merciful to everyone, there are other factors to consider. To begin with, what kind of precedent are you setting? Has the person shown true rehabilitation and prepared themselves for a different life? If they were guilty, have they repented and shown remorse? What about the victim and the victim's family? How will they be impacted by your decision?

Time after time, after being presented with the merits of a

particular case by our legal team, I would leave the meeting, saying, "I am going to need some time to think and pray about this one. This is a hard one." Most situations are more complicated than they at first appear.

AUGUST 6, 2019: "CYNTOIA WILL BE FREED"

On January 7, 2019, I announced that Cyntoia would be freed from prison on August 6, 2019. That would be fifteen years from the day she had shot Johnny Allen.

I decided to free Cyntoia for a lot of reasons. First, fifteen years is the sentence a juvenile would probably receive under today's sentencing guidelines. Second, while her crime was horrific, her circumstances as a victim of sex trafficking were not to be minimized. Finally, and most importantly in my mind, Cyntoia had become the picture of a redeemed life. The rehabilitation that we hope happens with incarceration had happened in her life. It had been a long and broken road, but her journey had become a story of change, and I was convinced that society was better with Cyntoia out of prison rather than with her spending at least another thirty-six years inside the prison walls.

Every now and then we get a view of the tapestry that God is weaving together in this world. For me, one of those times occurred when God intersected my life with Cyntoia Brown, now Cyntoia Brown Long after her marriage to Jaime Long. Although we were born less than two hundred miles away from each other, it is hard to imagine two lives being less similar.

I am a white guy from East Tennessee who grew up in a loving, two-parent family of considerable means. I had access to great education and a stable home environment and never spent a day in any kind of prison or state institution. Cyntoia grew up as the adopted biracial daughter of African American parents in middle Tennessee. A victim of sexual abuse on multiple occasions, she was in and out of several state institutions before she shot Johnny Allen.

In February 2019, after we had left office but before she had been released from prison, Crissy and I went to the Tennessee Prison for Women to meet Cyntoia for the first time. While Crissy and I had visited numerous prisons during our time in office, this was the first time we had ever been to a prison to visit a specific person. And not just any person, but someone with whom we had shared a story for the last six months, even though we had never met. Cyntoia had spent most of the last year wondering and praying about the decision I would make about her future. I had spent a lot of time reading about her and praying about the right decision in a case that had attracted so much attention.

When the three of us finally met in a small room at the prison, it was not the meeting of a woman who had spent her entire adult life in prison and a former governor and first lady. It felt more like a family reunion between relatives who knew all about each other but had never met. It was fascinating for us to hear what she had been thinking and wondering in the months when we were deliberating about her future and her name was trending on social media.

The story of her search for redemption and freedom is a beautiful story of a God who changes lives. The story of how her life intersected with my role as governor is a story of a God of mercy and justice who calls us also to be people of mercy and justice, even when it is not always clear how we can do both at the same time.

ACTORS IN A DRAMA

In all our stories, we realize that there are other actors in the drama, but we do not always get to watch their scenes. The choices we make, regardless of our positions, often affect other people's lives, even though we sometimes do not see it. When Crissy and I met Cyntoia, we were all in the same room together, and for the first time we were able to listen and learn about how our lives have intersected.

Though our backgrounds, experiences, and perspectives were very different, Cyntoia, Crissy, and I shared something more than just playing different roles in the same story. All three of us serve a God who believes in justice and mercy. All three of us need that mercy for things we have done and said and thought. And all three of us are grateful that the God of mercy and justice calls us his children, despite the things we have done. All of us need that justice and that mercy before entering the public square.

The day we sat with Cyntoia was a wonderful reminder of Paul's words that "there is neither Jew nor Greek, there is neither slave nor free, there is no male and female, for you are all one in Christ Jesus" (Galatians 3:28).

As we continue to look at how we bring a faithful presence into the public square, let's build on the knowledge that all distinctions fall away in the kingdom of God. Even distinctions between those who could grant clemency and those who have to wait to receive clemency. And, as Christians who have received clemency for our own shortcomings and failures, we should walk into that public square with humility and a keen awareness of being forgiven.

11

MY LIFE IN THE ARENA

I hope you are beginning to agree with me that, though it might look different for all of us, we all should have a presence in the public square. Perhaps it is running for office, or maybe it is being a well-informed citizen who takes seriously his or her responsibility to advocate and vote. Decisions made in the public arena are too important and impact too many citizens for people of faith to focus on only one issue or to not be involved at all. For me, I am confident that I never would have run for office if it were not for my faith.

I spent the first twenty-two years after college in business, though I never really intended to do that. I had studied history in college with a plan to teach high school for a couple of years and then go to seminary to be a pastor. But as I was preparing to graduate from college, my father approached me with a different thought. He said that if I really wanted to be a pastor in the long run, perhaps my time would be better served in business, rather than teaching, before going to seminary. That way, when I was a pastor, I would be better prepared to identify with people from the business world. That made sense to me. So I changed my plans and went to work for Pilot Corporation, the business my father had started the year I was born.

I began working there in the summer of 1980. A year later, Crissy and I were married. During the two years I thought would be a precursor to going to seminary, I became involved in our local church. After we were married, Crissy and I visited several seminaries to begin the process of deciding where to attend in the fall of 1982. As much as I loved being involved with our church and other ministries, and as interesting as I found our seminary visits, I began to sense that I was not called to be a pastor. When it came time to actually send my applications, I was convinced it was not the right path. I decided to stay for one more year at Pilot.

Life in the world of business moved on. The one more year turned into another and then another and then twenty. Our three children, Will, Annie, and Leigh, were born, and our lives revolved around raising our family—a time Crissy and I loved and fully embraced. The business was growing rapidly, doubling in size every three or four years and expanding from a regional convenience store company to a national truck stop chain. All the while, we remained very involved in our church and with our local Young Life committee as well as in other community roles.

Yet, in the same way that I knew I was not supposed to be a pastor, I also knew that working at Pilot was not going to be my lifelong career. I had a growing desire to do something else, though I didn't know what that other thing would be. After twenty years at Pilot, I left to help start the internet retail business for Saks Fifth Avenue. If you are wondering what selling high fashion on the internet has to do with running a truck stop chain, that is a really good question! I knew very little about the growing phenomenon of internet retailing, and even less about fashion. But these were the pioneer days of internet retailing, and most people were learning as they went too, so I fit right in. These were the days when anything with a dot-com at the end of its name was an explosive growth stock.

As interesting as that experience was, I knew it also was not what I wanted to do long term. In 2001, some friends in Knoxville approached me with the idea of running for mayor in 2003. I literally laughed when they brought up the idea. When I told them they had the wrong man, they asked if I would at least think and pray about it. It is a little hard to tell someone you will not even think and pray about their idea. So I began to do that. And I brought the idea up to my Friday Five, the four other guys I had been meeting with to pray and study the Bible on Friday mornings for almost twenty years. To my surprise, they thought it was an idea worth pursuing.

A month later, I was on spring break with my kids in Florida. Though we had not planned it, an old friend of mine, Bob Corker, was staying two doors down with his family for spring break as well. Bob and I had been friends for more than twenty-five years, from the time he and my brother were roommates in college. He had recently left a successful real estate development business to become the mayor of Chattanooga and would later serve two terms in the US Senate. Since we are both bike riders, we agreed to meet one morning for a twenty-mile bike ride. Somehow, during our conversation on that twenty-mile ride, I went from thinking that running for mayor of Knoxville was a crazy idea to thinking that maybe I should seriously consider running. After a few more months of thinking, discussing, and praying, in September 2002, I announced that I would run in the 2003 election.

I won. Barely. I have been a candidate on six different election nights, all of them exciting in their own way. But I will never forget the first one and having to wait until the last precinct was counted before we knew the outcome.

Much to my surprise, I discovered I loved being mayor. As a matter of fact, after a couple of years, I told people that this was the first time I understood what it was like to feel called to a role. I felt like everything I had done in the past had taught and prepared me for this job. I went into the role thinking I would be the CEO of the city, but it felt much more like being the senior pastor to the city. Not so I could deliver a sermon to the city, but so I could serve a diverse group of people with varying ideas about what the city should do and be; much like a pastor serves a diverse church with different pictures of what the church should do and be.

I was reelected in fall 2007, my last allowed term as mayor. In 2010, there was going to be an election for an open governor seat in Tennessee. Because being mayor had felt like such a calling for me, in 2008, I once again went through the process of thinking, discussing, and praying about running for governor. I had mixed emotions. I truly had loved being mayor and was intrigued by the idea of doing a similar job on a larger scale. But I knew it would be a long campaign (almost two years), and it would be a particularly hard-fought Republican primary. It also meant I would leave my role as mayor a year early if I won and would be on the road campaigning the year before that.

The political trend at the time would favor whatever Republican emerged from the primary. Tennessee has a history of the governor's office alternating between Republican and Democrat, and the current governor was a Democrat. It had been almost fifty years since an incoming governor had replaced someone of the same party. It would also be the first midterm election of the Obama presidency, and midterms are historically difficult for the party in power. Finally, Tennessee was trending Republican, as more and more of our rural citizens switched from blue to red. All of this meant there would be several eager and viable Republicans competing in the primary.

After about six months of thinking, talking, and praying about it, Crissy and I decided that we were called to run. However, we also said that we would not run if Senator Bill

Frist decided to enter the race. Senator Frist is a former heart surgeon who had become majority leader of the US Senate and left after serving two terms. He was seriously considering running for governor, and we had many of the same supporters. He had also been helpful to me a number of times while I was mayor, and I wanted to honor him. I can honestly say that I felt more called to run for governor than I felt eager to run. So I still remember the sick feeling in my stomach when Senator Frist called me the day after Christmas in 2008 to say that he was not going to run for governor. I hung up the phone, turned to Crissy, and said, "I guess we are supposed to run for governor now."

As the campaign stretched out over almost two years, it was, at times, as difficult as I suspected it might be. But there was never a moment when Crissy or I did not believe that we were right where God had called us to be. I don't think we will ever forget the moment all the news organizations announced that we had won. Election nights are a combination of excitement and relief. But they are primarily a confirmation that there is a next part of the political journey.

Like being mayor, I found that serving as governor felt more like a calling than anything I had ever done. And I quickly learned that being a mayor and being in business were both great preparation for being a governor. It felt like one more time in my life when God had a path for me that I never would have selected but I am glad I did not miss.

While the primary contest was much more competitive and winning it was exciting, winning the general election changed my life really quickly. When you are running for office, the object is to meet with as many people as you can. If anyone will listen, the candidate is ready and willing to meet with them. I joked during the campaign that "where two or three are gathered," I wanted to be there. The minute you are elected, everything changes.

Now, everyone wants to talk to you. Suddenly, countless people want to meet the new governor. Everyone has a cause that needs to be understood or a relative who needs to be hired. You need to hire your staff and twenty-three commissioners to head each of the departments of state government. And there is an inauguration to plan and your first state budget to prepare and present to the legislature within weeks of taking office. The real challenge, though, is setting your priorities with hundreds of competing causes and needs battling for attention.

ENDLESS NEEDS

The needs and opportunities for change are almost endless when you are in office. Yet the time and dollars needed to make those changes and meet those needs are limited. With so many people and legitimate needs pulling in multiple directions, prioritizing them is both more difficult and more important than in a business setting where everyone agrees on the main mission of the business.

Unlike the clear biblical call for humility and meekness we discussed earlier, policy and priority decisions can rarely be defined as a clear call from God. Scripture is unambiguous about some things like justice, mercy, compassion, and humility. But the policies and priorities meant to accomplish those objectives are less defined. That's why there is room for differences among Christians when it comes to policies, priorities, and political parties. My views on government and my decisions on policies are impacted and informed by my faith, but that does not mean my specific policy decisions are the only ones Christians can make. Likewise, my three key priorities were not the only legitimate needs that could have been prioritized. They were simply what I felt was important to highlight in my desire to be faithful to my calling.

My first priority was to make sure state government worked for our citizens. Because in most cases state government is a monopoly—for example, if you need a driver's license, the state is your only option—it has a real responsibility to deliver the best service it can for the lowest cost in taxes. While I was in office, Tennessee's state budget was $38 billion annually, and we had forty thousand state employees. While a lot of political campaigns focus on social issues, and even a candidate's position on national issues, I always thought that our primary job was to serve the 6.6 million citizens who called Tennessee home. We helped educate kindergarten kids and PhD candidates. We helped families with mental health issues, built interstate highways, served our disabled citizens, provided protective custody for abused children, deployed National Guard troops around the world, and so much more. We also tried to keep your wait time at the DMV from lasting longer than your patience. We did better at some things than others.

All of us, Republican and Democrat, should focus more on making government work better. Government matters, and good government can make a big difference. Conservatives have often thought of government as the problem, not the answer, in Ronald Reagan's famous words. Liberals have too often thought that more money was the answer to most problems. My view is that government is like fire. Out of control, fire can cause a lot of damage. Under control, it can warm our rooms and cook our meals. All of us need government to work, for our lives to work, regardless of our income level. No one can buy their own interstate system or an army to protect them against threats. The same is true for a child welfare system, health department, corrections system, and many other essential government services.

I have always felt that the key to giving great service to citizens, like giving great service to customers, is to have great people on your team. I have already written about how we reformed the civil service system so that we hired and promoted the most qualified and best performing instead of just using seniority as the measurement. We also worked to change our compensation model. The old model was: "Come to work for the government. Our pay is mediocre at best. Everyone will get the same raise, regardless of how good a job you do. But your job is safe and pretty much guaranteed for life, and we have really good long-term benefits." There is no part of that model that says we want people to focus on delivering great service. So we increased the average employee pay by over ten thousand dollars. We also put in a performance-based payment system that rewarded employees who did good work. And we made sure everyone had a performance review two times a year so they would have opportunities to improve and grow.

My second priority was public education. While some citizens could afford private schools, the vast majority were educated in our public schools. From kindergarten to graduate school, for citizens to have the chance at a life-changing education, the state had to focus relentlessly on improving the quality of our schools.

Doing that was more difficult than I ever dreamed. When we talk about great schools, a lot of issues come up. How do parents feel about the education their child is receiving? What do teachers have to say about the programs and policies of the schools? How much money are we spending on education? All those things, and many more, are important. But they pale in comparison to these two basic questions: Are our children and adult learners experiencing better outcomes? Are they learning what they need to learn?

There have been a lot of conversations about income inequality in our country. Deservedly so. Regardless of your politics, the numbers show that the income gap is real and increasing. Therefore, the question becomes, What are we going to do about it? In Tennessee, we determined that an increasing percentage of our jobs were requiring a post-secondary degree or certificate, which meant students would have to have that credential to compete for those quality jobs in the future. But too many of our citizens thought they were not "college material" or that they could not afford college. We needed to change the culture of expectation and the conversations around dinner tables about college all across the state. So we launched the Tennessee Promise, becoming the first state to promise everyone two years of free college at our community colleges and technical schools.

The response was dramatic. Our college attendance rate soared. We saw big increases in applications from low-income students and from "first-generation students," those who were the first in their families to attend college.

I know the difference it can make on an individual to have the opportunity to go to college. Crissy and I are both children of first-generation college students, and I know the trajectory-changing impact that college can have in a person's life. I also know that access to college is only the first step. It is success at college that really matters—it is completing college, not just starting college, that really changes lives.

Being successful in college means being prepared when you get there. And being prepared when you get there means you need to have had access to high-quality, rigorous education in your K–12 years. That means not accepting the idea that some kids in some neighborhoods with some backgrounds can't learn. It means insisting on high standards for what a child should learn each step of the way, and some kind of measurement to see how much they have learned in each grade.

Those are the changes Tennessee enacted so we would become the fastest-improving state in the country in education. A lot of people deserve credit for that. Teachers and parents did the hard work every day. My predecessor, Phil Bredesen, and a lot of courageous legislators made difficult decisions and prodded Tennesseans to aim higher. But the heart of the progress was the result of the idea that "all means all" when it comes to providing *all* children with a quality education. And that high academic standards, along with a way to measure what students have learned, are critical to the effort. The longer I was in office, the more I became convinced that demanding high-quality public education for all kids is an equity issue and a justice issue.

Often your priorities are determined by the times in which you lead and serve. When I came into office, Tennessee and the rest of the country were still recovering from the impact of the Great Recession of 2008 and 2009. Unemployment rates were at 10.5 percent in Tennessee. Manufacturing jobs were leaking away to other places and were no longer providing a path to a middle-class life. All those factors led me to make job recruitment my third priority.

This was a fun and interesting part of being the governor. Having spent years in business, I understood the language and issues facing companies that were choosing a location for their business. It also fit me philosophically. As essential as government can be, I believe there is very little that serves a family as well as a quality job. I felt our work at the state was to provide an environment where businesses would have confidence in putting their capital at risk.

To me, it is all a linked circle. The connection between a healthy job market and high-quality education is direct and undeniable. Today's highly automated economy means it will take fewer people to perform most tasks, but those people will also require more training. We launched Tennessee Promise so more people could be prepared for the coming jobs and Tennessee would be an attractive place for companies to invest their capital. Without that, too many people would be left out of the changing economy. We had to provide access to higher education, particularly for those families who were at risk of being left behind. But, circling back around, the access to higher education would not serve anyone well if they were not prepared when they got there. So we had to relentlessly go back to the beginning and talk about an education approach for our K-12 programs that was measured by better outcomes for students.

While my priorities might have been education, jobs, and more effective government services, other issues always found their way to me. There were 132 other elected officials serving in the Tennessee legislature, each with their own ideas, constituents, and microphones. There were forest fires on Thanksgiving Day and tornadoes on Christmas Eve, when tornadoes are not supposed to hit. It is a sobering moment to stand with a family and look out at their entire life's possessions strewn across the hillside, including the presents their kids were supposed to have opened the next morning.

Some responsibilities I welcomed, like the chance to appoint judges. I know how important it is to have a fair and impartial judicial system, and I was honored to get to play a part in the process. Other responsibilities felt heavy, and I would have rather not been a part of them. Chief among those was the governor's role in the capital punishment process.

I was motivated to run for governor for a lot of reasons. Being the last phone call made by the prison warden before a man was executed was not one of them. In theory, I knew that the governor was the last step in a lengthy process before a death sentence was carried out. But the reality of being in that position was very different.

The governor's role is to make certain that the process works; one last human check to affirm that the judicial system has not gone off track. I did not look at my role as the thirteenth juror to rehear the trial and all the evidence. Rather, my role was to make certain the convicted had proper representation, no new exculpatory evidence—like a new DNA test—had surfaced, and all methods of appeal had been exhausted.

My first seven and a half years in office, there were no executions scheduled. In my last half year, the Tennessee Supreme Court set three execution dates. In all three cases, the crimes had been committed more than thirty years earlier. As a Christian, I struggled with my personal view of the death penalty. I listened to persuasive arguments on both sides of the issue. And I read and listened to passionate arguments for the biblical position both for and against the death penalty. In all honesty, I remain unconvinced that there is a clear biblical position on the issue.

As a practical matter, the fact that the appeals process can last decades means that the execution usually occurs long after the crime. It is a long, expensive process for everyone involved, including the victim's family. The condemned person is subsequently a very different person by the time the sentence is carried out.

In all three cases, I declined to intervene in the process. All had been convicted by a jury of their peers. In each case, the defendant had made numerous appeals that were heard by multiple courts on the state and federal level. Our team could not find anywhere that the system had not worked the way it was designed to work. And, I had sworn to uphold the Constitution and the laws of the state.

All three times, we worked hard to make sure we knew everything we should and had considered everything before us. All three nights, Crissy and I waited by the phone before the execution to see if the Tennessee Supreme Court had issued a stay. All three times, I answered the call from the prison asking if I had anything to say. All three nights are forever fixed in my memory.

While those were the most difficult days of my time in office, there were other days of struggle and frustration. But there was never a day as mayor or governor when I did not feel honored to get to do the job. Every day, as I walked up the steps of the state capitol, I thought to myself, *I can't believe I get to do this.* When people would thank me for serving, I would usually reply, "Don't thank me. I have the best job in the country." We are all wired to want to make a difference. All of us want to feel like we are using the gifts we have to somehow make the world a little better. The beauty of public service is that your work gets leveraged because of all the things that government can do when it works the way it is supposed to work.

This is my story of how God chose to use me in the public arena. My story is not everyone's story. Truthfully, it was not all that long ago that I could have imagined this even being my story. I share it not as a plea for everyone to run for office but for all of us to see politics as a vocation, a place where, despite all of its messiness, God has used and will use faithful people.

It is also a plea for all of us to take seriously our role in the public arena. It does matter who we elect. Compassionate, purposeful government makes this world a better place. As frustrating as the process might be, it matters too much for people of faith to just check out of the process. Instead, with hearts set on civil and not cynical governing, we can bring humility, hope, and a commitment to getting to the best answer, not just our answer.

12

WHAT DOES A FAITHFUL PRESENCE LOOK LIKE?

For so much of this book, we've asked the questions: How do we live a life of faithful presence in the world we live in today? How should people of faith approach the public square in a way that draws people to Jesus rather than chases them away? How do we enter into the public square to serve, and still not "be conformed to this world, but be transformed by the renewal of your mind, that by testing you may discern what is the will of God, what is good and acceptable and perfect" (Romans 12:2)?

Now that I've shared a great deal of my journey with you, I hope you'll accept some practical points that, in my experience, help us build a faithful presence as citizens. These are things each of us can cultivate in ways both large and small, no matter who we are or what our role is. And it starts with simply showing up.

FAITHFUL PRESENCE BEGINS WITH PRESENCE

The first important step to having a faithful presence is to actually be present.

I wrote earlier about how I ended up running for public office. I kept coming back to this Bible passage during the time I was thinking and praying about running for mayor:

> Thus says the LORD of hosts, the God of Israel, to all the exiles whom I have sent into exile from Jerusalem to Babylon: Build houses and live in them; plant gardens and eat their produce.

161

Take wives and have sons and daughters; take wives for your sons, and give your daughters in marriage, that they may bear sons and daughters; multiply there, and do not decrease. But seek the welfare of the city where I have sent you into exile, and pray to the LORD on its behalf, for in its welfare you will find your welfare. (Jeremiah 29:4–7)

When I first heard a friend of mine, Pastor Doug Banister, preach on this passage, I could not believe the advice that Jeremiah was giving the Israelites. The Jewish people were being held captive in a horrible place. If I were ever held captive by an evil regime, I'd hope the authority figure back home would write saying that they were coming to get me as quickly as possible.

Some historical background here is helpful. Nebuchadnezzar had conquered Jerusalem and enslaved the Israelites. He had dragged most of the Jews, including the skilled craftsmen and almost all the priests and leaders, back to Babylon, almost a thousand miles away from Jerusalem. He had not only taken most of their possessions but also desecrated the temple. Nebuchadnezzar's ego was even greater than his power. While he built monuments to himself with his name on all the bricks, his people lived in poverty. Given that he treated his own people that way, it is safe to say that the Israelites were treated even worse.

Jeremiah's message to the captured Jews was not an encouraging one:

Get used to it. You are going to be there a while. You will be captive through the time of Nebuchadnezzar, as well as his son and grandson (Jeremiah 25:11; 27:7; 29:10), a period that will last more than seventy years. Also, don't count on the remnant of Jews who were left in Jerusalem to come and save you. Get used to the fact that this is going to be home for a long time.

It must have been hard for the Israelites to hear Jeremiah say that it was God who had carried them into exile, not Nebuchadnezzar. But Jeremiah's message didn't just stop there. He also made it clear that it was Babylon where God was at work now—and exile was the role God had chosen for Israel for several generations. This was why he told them to build and plant and marry and have children. They were in it for the long haul, so to speak, and he was calling them to take part in his work, even while in exile.

MOVE BEYOND ANGER, WITHDRAWAL, OR ASSIMILATION

Today, it is easy for people of faith to feel that we are under siege. As the culture seems to change and deteriorate, our reaction has frequently been to strike back in anger or to withdraw into our own huddles. Or, knowingly or unknowingly, to decide it is easier just to be like everyone else.

James Davison Hunter is a University of Virginia professor who coined the term *faithful presence* that I have used as the title for this book. In his book *To Change the World*, Hunter writes that it would have been natural for the Jews to react in many of the same ways that we have to their changed circumstances.

Clearly it would have been justifiable for the Jews to be *hostile* to their captors. It also would have been natural enough for them to *withdraw* from engaging the world around them. By the same token, it would have been easy for them to simply *assimilate* with the culture that surrounded them. . . . But God was calling them to something different—not to be defensive against, isolated from, or absorbed into the dominant culture, but to be faithfully present within it.[1] (emphasis added)

We cannot react out of *hostility* to those who differ from us politically when we are supposed to love our enemies. If we are going to have a faithful presence, that presence cannot be marked by fear of our changing circumstances and anger at the people who think differently than we do.

We also cannot *withdraw* into our own homes or churches. It would have been natural for the Jews to withdraw from the world around them. Babylon was certainly nothing like Jerusalem, and it would have been comforting to look inward into their own community, where it was still as faithful a world that it could be, with people who had similar understandings of things. But faithful presence means we are called to bring the *shalom* of God to places where God has called us, with the gifts that God has given us. It is hard to be a faithful presence when we have retreated to our own safe places.

Finally, we cannot just *assimilate* to the culture around us. It had to be tempting for the Jews to consider becoming like the Babylonians. After all, God had told them to settle in, plant gardens, and build houses. It would've been easy to become just like the rest of the neighborhood. But God was calling them to something harder. He was asking them to keep their distinctiveness as God's people as they entered into a hostile community, but to do it in a way that made the community a better place for everyone. That is a tough assignment.

Then Jeremiah told the Jews to do something that had to

seem crazy for captives to do for their captors. He told them to seek the welfare of the Babylonians. Not only that, they were to pray for these people who ransacked their city, destroyed their temple, and enslaved them. Why? Because the Israelites' welfare was tied up with the Babylonians' welfare. Being faithfully present meant they were to be a blessing right in the place where God had called them, even if it was a thousand miles from home and under the thumb of merciless captors.

The New Testament frequently echoes the language of Jeremiah. Peter and Paul referred to the early Christians as "exiles," "aliens," and "strangers." In his letter to the Galatians, Paul referred to the times as "the present evil age" (1:4). Yet, despite being exiles in an evil age, Paul told the Galatians, "So then, as we have opportunity, let us do good to everyone, and especially to those who are of the household of faith" (6:10). Don't miss the *everyone* in the rush to see *especially to those who are of the household of faith*.

CONSIDER IT EVERYBODY'S NEIGHBORHOOD

When I was elected mayor of Knoxville, one of the biggest challenges for the city was that everyone had begun to think of themselves as citizens of the part of the city where they lived—East, West, South, and North Knoxville—rather than thinking of the city as a whole. There were some legitimate historical reasons for that. Resentment and distrust had led to disagreements large and small between the various areas of town.

My primary focus as mayor was to reinvigorate our downtown. Like a lot of center cities, Knoxville's downtown had deteriorated as people moved to the suburbs over the previous fifty years. Prioritizing downtown made sense for a lot of reasons. The infrastructure was all in place, making it easier to turn abandoned buildings into productive businesses, which meant increased tax collections for the city. Growth in the central part of the city also meant that we weren't fighting over who got the commercial real estate near their neighborhoods. But the most important reason to promote downtown had nothing to do with the financial benefits for the city.

More than one hundred years before I was mayor, Market Square, the heart of downtown, was described in the *Knoxville Journal and Tribune* as "the most Democratic place on earth. There the rich and the poor, the white and the black, jostle each other in perfect equality."[2] The city needed a place like that where it was everybody's place because it was nobody's exclusive place.

We began to market downtown Knoxville as "everybody's neighborhood," and it became the preferred destination for entertainment, restaurants, and cultural events for people of all ages, neighborhoods, and backgrounds. We also encouraged people to live downtown to add a constant energy to the area. People from all over the region, as well as tourists, began coming to the new restaurants and stores. Entertainment spaces and even churches sprang up. Eventually people referred to themselves less as being from West, East, North, or South Knoxville. As downtown truly became everybody's neighborhood, the entire community took pride in the new identity of Knoxville.

Today, my office is in downtown Knoxville, and it gives me real joy to stroll through the area and see people from all parts of the city, and a lot of tourists, enjoying a flourishing downtown. It is a way that God allowed me to be a part of seeking the peace of the city where he had called me.

ACT JUSTLY, LOVE MERCY, WALK HUMBLY

About a hundred years before Jeremiah wrote to the captives in Babylon, the prophet Micah asked what the Lord required of us. He considered offering burnt offerings, thousands of rams, ten thousands of rivers of oil, and even his firstborn. But the answer to his question was something quite different, and it can be found in the familiar words of Micah 6:8: "He has told you, O man, what is good; and what does the LORD require of you but to do justice, and to love kindness, and to walk humbly with your God?"

The more I have seen of our problems, particularly the ones that seem the most intractable, the more convinced I am that acting justly, loving mercy, and walking humbly are our only hope for real change. *But the change will happen only if we are doing all three of those things at the same time.* Pursuing justice without mercy will lead only to self-righteousness. Mercy without justice leaves unaddressed many of the inequities that plague us today. And, justice or mercy without humility results in a destructive pride about how just and merciful we are.

The reason Cyntoia Brown's case from chapter 10 struck such a deep part of me was because of that sense of wanting to do justice and mercy at the same time yet struggling with how to do that. All of us want justice when someone has taken something from us. When people participate in a protest march, they are calling for justice over an inequity. Our court system is supposed to correct wrongs, and we expect our justice system to do that.

Christians should be in the middle of that fight for justice. C. S. Lewis described it this way:

For Christianity is a fighting religion. It thinks God made the world. . . . But it also thinks that a great many things have gone wrong with the world that God made and that God insists, and insists very loudly, on our putting them right again.[3]

Yes, we want justice. But we also know we need mercy. Just as Christians should be leading in fighting for justice, we should be leading the pack in showing mercy. We of all people should understand mercy, since we understand that God has granted us such great mercy.

In Matthew 18, Jesus tells a great story about a king who decides to settle accounts with his servants. One servant owes the king a large sum, but when he is brought before the king to settle, he begs the king to be patient with him and promises to pay his debts in full. The king has pity on him and decides to not only release him but also forgive his debt. This same servant, freshly forgiven of his debts, then goes to demand payment of a debt he is owed from a fellow servant. When his fellow servant cannot pay, the forgiven servant has him thrown in prison. When the king hears what has happened, he says, "You wicked servant! I forgave you all that debt because you pleaded with me. And should not you have had mercy on your fellow servant, as I had mercy on you?" (vv. 32–33). Having been shown such great mercy, we are now called to show mercy in return.

I wrote earlier about humility and the reasons "God opposes the proud but gives grace to the humble" (1 Peter 5:5; James 4:6). Humility means that we get it. "For by grace you have been saved through faith. And this is not your own doing; it is the gift of God, not a result of works, so that no one may boast" (Ephesians 2:8–9). I truly believe that our most difficult conversations about our deepest differences would have entirely different results if they were approached with humility.

Christians are uniquely equipped to address the issues that seem so difficult to solve. Racism, economic opportunity, equity in education, taking care of creation, and our long-term debt challenges are just some of the issues that need to be viewed through a lens of justice, mercy, and humility. Think how different those conversations would be if they were directed by those three key attributes instead of our need to win the argument. Because we serve a God of justice, a God who said, "Let justice roll down like waters" (Amos 5:24), we, too, should be committed to justice. Having received such gracious mercy ourselves, we have the capacity to give mercy. And, knowing that the story is not about us, but that we are part of a larger story that God is writing, we can humbly look to see where God might use us without worrying about who gets the credit.

SPEAK THE TRUTH WITH LOVE

I know a lot of people who take pride in being "truth tellers." You know them too. They are the ones who are quick to proudly proclaim, "I tell it like it is." But no one ever feels very loved around them. Others love well but have a hard time ever landing on a spot from which they cannot be moved. They are the ones Paul described in Ephesians as "tossed to and fro by the waves and carried about by every wind of doctrine, by human cunning, by craftiness in deceitful schemes" (4:14).

So what is the balance between the two? How do we hold both truth and love in tension?

Our times are often described as postmodern. Postmodernism

is the idea that truth is subject to change and open to individual determination. The spirit of the age says what is true for you might not be true for me. While this is typically thought of as a product of the second half of the twentieth century, Pontius Pilate delivered the signature phrase of postmodernism back at the beginning of the first century.

After Jesus was arrested earlier in the night, he was brought for trial before Pilate, the governor of the Roman province of Judea. As Pilate was interrogating Jesus, he asked, "So you are a king?" Jesus replied, "You say that I am a king. For this purpose I was born and for this purpose I have come into the world—to bear witness to the truth. Everyone who is of the truth listens to my voice" (John 18:37). Pilate's response, "What is truth?" (v. 38), would fit in well in our postmodern world. Jesus said he came into the world to bear witness to the truth. Pilate, probably having heard a lot of arguments in his role as governor, had given up on the idea of truth.

I was teaching a class at Vanderbilt when a student stopped me in the middle of a discussion and asked if I believed there was such a thing as truth that was true for everyone. She was surprised when I said I did. She was even more surprised when I said I thought she did too. I pointed out that her backpack and laptop were both covered with pins and stickers demanding rights for various groups. If there is no such thing as transcendent truth—truth that is true regardless of the situation—then where does the idea of "rights" come from? If truth is relative and dependent on the situation, then it is hard to claim that moral rights exist.

Jesus does not give us the alternative of deciding what may be true for you might not be true for me. "I am the way, and the truth, and the life" (John 14:6) is about as far away from a postmodern statement on truth as you can get. Likewise, he does not give us the alternative of deciding who we will love.

The well-known passage on love from 1 Corinthians 13 has become best known for being read at weddings. As the loving couple stands at the altar, we all nod our heads as the reader reminds us that love is patient and kind; it does not envy or boast; it is not arrogant or rude; it does not insist on its own way; it is not irritable or resentful; and it does not rejoice at wrongdoing but rejoices with the truth. The hard part is when we are reminded that Paul did not write that passage for wedding ceremonies but for all of life, including politics.

We are clearly called to love our fellow believers: "By this all people will know that you are my disciples, if you have love for one another" (John 13:35). But that is the easy part. He also tells us that we are to love even those we don't like and those who are on a different political side, when he says "love your enemies" (Matthew 5:44). It's not an either-or type of situation when it comes to truth and love. It's a both-and.

DEMOCRACY IN TROUBLE

There is a strong consensus that American democracy is in trouble. I have cited statistics throughout this book that show our country's growing sense of animosity and contempt between the Left and the Right. Most of us don't need those statistics to tell us what we already know: distrust between the players in the public square is at toxic levels. Citizens also seem to have a mounting suspicion that we are no longer capable of solving our biggest challenges. Sadly, very few look to people of faith to help bridge the divide and solve our biggest problems.

I think it is for a time like this that Christians are called to the public square, but not in the ways that we have traditionally approached it. These times call out for people who understand that our cries for justice have to be accompanied by a humble and merciful spirit. These times require citizens who are committed to both truth and love, not one without the other. We can be people who truly seek the peace of the places we have been exiled, knowing that God has tied our welfare to the welfare of the places he has called us.

13

A FEW EXAMPLES AND WHY IT MATTERS

Earlier I told my story of how my faith led me into the public square. There are far better examples than mine of how faith has shaped and improved our country. As we think about what a faithful presence might look like, it is helpful to know we have many people who have gone before us. And, because many today would deny that faith should have any role in our public discussions, it is helpful to think about how different our country might be without that faithful presence.

HARRIET TUBMAN

Harriet Tubman is still known today because of her courage as a conductor of the Underground Railroad—the network of safe houses set up to help slaves escape to free states or Canada. Tubman was born into slavery in Dorchester County, Maryland. Hearing that she was about to be sold to another owner, she pulled off a daring escape to a safe house in Philadelphia. Remarkably, Tubman returned to guide numerous others to freedom. The terminus for many of the Underground Railroad journeys was in Saint Catharines, Ontario, at Salem Chapel, which was also her home church.

Today, many people visit the chapel because of its historical connection to Tubman. On your visit, you will be greeted by a letter from the church trustees:

Dear Reader,

We wish to express our thanks to you for your interest in our most famous member, Harriet Tubman, and the African American freedom seekers who built the Salem Chapel and their connection to the legendary Underground Railroad. We too are just as enthusiastic, if not more so, because we are the guardians of their honourable memory and custodians of the church. However, it is important that you know that our first priority is to serve our Lord and Saviour, Jesus Christ, because that is what we believe Sister Tubman and all other past members would want us to do.

We realize that this may be difficult for some of you to understand and that some of you may disagree with us, however, please recognize that this is our position and it is also our prerogative. There will be no argument relating to this matter, because we understand that our forefathers built the church to praise the Lord, not themselves. We also do not believe that they would want us to place them above God.

We believe that the only time Sister Tubman would have missed attending a Sunday Worship Service, whether she was in the US or Canada, is when she was guiding fugitives to freedom or if she was ill. No matter what the Sunday circumstances may have been, we believe that Sister Tubman would have taken the time to give thanks to the Lord as she did on a daily basis.

The Salem Chapel is a functional church, and we do hold a public worship service every Sunday, therefore, we operate very differently from a museum, interpretive centre, etc., because our first priority is to serve the Lord. . . .

Peace be with you and God bless,
Salem Chapel NHS Trustees[1]

The trustees of Salem Chapel seem intent on not only celebrating the lives of Tubman and her fellow church members but also reminding us all of what motivated their actions. Tubman herself would respond to praise of her actions with, "Twant me, twas the Lord. I always told him, 'I trust to you. I don't know where to go or what to do, but I expect you to lead me', and he always did."[2]

WILLIAM WILBERFORCE

The American fight against slavery had a role model from across the ocean in England's William Wilberforce. In the late 1700s, economic motivations in the British Empire for slavery were so strong that a publicist for one West Indies Trade wrote, "The impossibility of doing without slaves in the West Indies will always prevent this traffic being dropped."[3] Only a small group of people thought slavery could ever be ended in the British Empire. Wilberforce was one of those people.

He was an unlikely crusader against slavery or anything else. Born into a life of privilege, he later said of his own youth, "As much pains were taken to make me idle as were ever taken to make me studious."[4] He was, however, politically motivated and succeeded in being elected to Parliament in 1780 at the age of twenty-one. He would later confess that "the first years in Parliament I did nothing—nothing to any purpose. My own distinction was my darling object."[5] That sounds familiar in today's world, where so many politicians seem to be primarily interested in self-promotion.

His life would change on Easter 1786 when he had a spiritual rebirth. Thinking he should quit politics and go into the ministry, Wilberforce was persuaded by John Newton, the writer of "Amazing Grace" and a former slave trader himself, that he could serve God by staying in Parliament. He now had a different view of his purpose: "My walk is a public one. My business is in this world and I must mix in the assemblies of men or quit the post which Providence seems to have assigned me."[6]

Wilberforce turned his efforts to ending slavery, the cause that would become his life's work. He faced powerful opposition from within Parliament, from the royal family, and from the multitudes that had a vested interest in slavery continuing. He first introduced legislation against the slave trade in 1789, only to have his twelve resolutions defeated. He would lose again in 1791, 1792, 1793, 1797, 1798, 1799, 1804, and 1805.

I know what it is like to have a legislative proposal fail. I am not sure I could have kept persisting. Yet he persisted, even though, during most of that time, he suffered from debilitating illnesses that left him bedridden for weeks at a time. Only three days before he died, in 1833, did he hear the news that the final passage of the emancipation bill was ensured in Parliament, more than thirty years before America would take the same overdue step. But for Wilberforce's spiritual awakening fifty years earlier, it might have been even longer before the British ended slavery in its empire.

MARTIN LUTHER KING JR. AND THE CIVIL RIGHTS MOVEMENT

In more recent times, it is impossible to picture the civil rights movement without the openly religious appeals of the Rev. Dr. Martin Luther King Jr. From his position as the leader of the Southern Christian Leadership Conference (SCLC), King spoke in deeply biblical language. His calls for justice and freedom were based on scriptural calls for justice and freedom.

King's "Letter from a Birmingham Jail" is recognized as one of the most important documents in our history. Written to his fellow clergymen who had argued that he should be more patient in his expectation of change, King's handwritten six-thousand-word letter was an argument for our moral responsibility to obey just laws and disobey unjust laws. To the key question of how we know the difference between just laws and unjust laws, King answered, "A just law is a man-made code that squares with the moral law or the law of God. An unjust law is a code that is out of harmony with the moral law."[7] For him, it always came back to God.

The same was true of thousands of black people, facing water hoses, police dogs, and repeated arrests, that captured the nation's attention. For many of them, the conviction that God was on their side reinforced their belief that their cause was just and mighty. They would not have dreamed of putting their quest in secular terms. Representative John Lewis died in 2020 after a long life of service and leadership in the civil rights movement. In a 2004 interview on PBS he said, "I'm deeply concerned that many people today fail to recognize that the movement was built on deep-seated religious convictions, and the movement grew out of a sense of faith—faith in God and faith in one's fellow human beings."[8]

GEORGE W. BUSH

George W. Bush led the global fight against AIDS, particularly battling the epidemic in Africa, where millions died from the disease. Bush, motivated by his own spiritual journey, launched PEPFAR, President's Emergency Plan for AIDS Relief, which is credited with saving millions of lives in Africa, when there wasn't a lot of political motivation to invest the time and resources to do that. After all, I doubt the issue of ending AIDS in Africa polled near the top of the issues that influenced voters in America. For Bush, it was part of what he felt was his reason for being in office.

All of us who serve in office have a few things that leave us thinking, *I am really glad I had the chance to do this while I was in office.* For Bush, helping to end the AIDS crisis in Africa was one of those things. It even launched an unlikely friendship and a relationship of mutual respect with the rock star Bono, who was motivated to be a part of the effort as a result of his own spiritual journey. I am pretty confident that Bono and Bush would typically have a different political view of the world. Yet, motivated by their faith, they helped to save countless lives.[9]

REASONABLE PEOPLE IN UNREASONABLE PLACES

New York Times columnist Nicholas Kristof once wrote a column about Dr. Tom Catena, who was the only doctor at the 435-bed Mother of Mercy Hospital in the Nuba Mountains of southern Sudan. He worked in a medical facility with very little medical equipment, while the Sudanese government dropped bombs around them, trying to wipe out a rebellion. The hospital had no electricity or running water. Kristof quotes "Dr. Tom," saying that he remained there for a particular reason: "So I see it as an obligation, as a Christian and as a human being, to help."[10]

Kristof goes on to say, "But the people I've encountered over the years in the most impossible places—like Nuba, where anyone reasonable has fled—are disproportionately unreasonable because of their faith."[11] Although Catena was a doctor operating in a remote part of the world rather than an elected official, I love the idea of choosing to walk into situations where "anyone reasonable has fled."

Many people would say that the public arena today is a place where reasonable people should flee. Thankfully, God continues to call reasonable people to unreasonable places.

The stories could go on and on. Yet many people would insist that the public square is not the place to bring our religious beliefs. After all, they would argue, the wall of separation between church and state is fundamental to American constitutional law. Therefore, we should separate our own faith from our political discussions and actions. The argument would go on to include the premise that bringing religious language into the discussion is not helpful since that language isn't universally accepted, or even known, among the rest of the population. John Rawls, one of the most influential political philosophers of the twentieth century, argued that religion is one of the many prejudices thoughtful citizens should leave behind when they enter the public square: "In public reason ideas of truth or right based on comprehensive doctrines [Rawls's term for religion] are replaced by an idea of the politically reasonable addressed to citizens as citizens."[12] In other words, lose the religious language when you come into the public square because all of us don't use that language.

Today, you hear that philosophy whenever you hear a politician say that something is "my personal religious view, but I would never impose my view on anyone else." While, as I've said previously, I firmly believe in the idea of not having a state-established religion, I have never understood how someone could say anything other than that their faith is the foundational truth for not just what they believe but also their political actions. There is a world of difference between the state establishing religion and individuals using their faith as a motivation for action. If not for that difference, our country would have missed the benefit of years of sacrificial service from people who were motivated to act because of what they believed.

George Will, the conservative commentator who describes himself as a "low-voltage, amiable atheist," said,

> The idea that I sometimes hear that religion has no place in public life—what country are they talking about? We were founded by people who came here for the free exercise of religion. We have a Constitution and a Declaration of Independence that radiate what the Judeo-Christian tradition has done for the world, which is to assert the primacy of the individual and the preciousness of the individual.[13]

Do the people who say religion should only be a private affair really want a world where the people of faith leave their faith at home? During a 2020 Democratic presidential debate, then candidate Beto O'Rourke proposed removing the tax exemption of any organization that did not support gay marriage. His candidacy ended soon after that, and his idea did not carry on past his campaign. But I am betting that the idea is not dead. Then, do we really want a world where we lose the goodness born of people of faith, as they are discouraged from bringing that faith to bear for the common good? An enormous number of hospitals, schools, and social service agencies have resulted from people of faith seeking to serve the least of these, and I wouldn't want to picture what our world would look like without them.

Many would answer that our actions to serve the common good are welcome; just don't bring all the rest of the baggage of your faith along with it. It is what Yale law professor Stephen Carter describes as "the tragedy of liberal theory when it meets religious commitment. The basic response of liberal theory to serious religion is to try to speak words that seem to celebrate it (as a part of the freedom of belief, or conscience, or the entitlement to select one's own version of the good) while in effect trying to domesticate it—or, if that fails, to try and destroy it."[14]

But the source of our motivations does matter. Religious communities that support acts of faith, whether it's the civil rights movement or community social service agencies, provide the courage, financial resources, and moral encouragement to keep going in difficult times. Often that comes from biblical encouragement to feed the hungry and heal the sick. And usually it comes from the biblical imperative to "not be conformed to this world, but be transformed by the renewal of your mind" (Romans 12:2).

ESTABLISHING A RELIGION VS. BEING MOTIVATED BY RELIGION: THE DIFFERENCE

In an earlier chapter, I made a defense of the idea that our government should not be used to establish a religion. I think the founders were particularly wise when they added that as part of the First Amendment to the Constitution. But there is all the difference in the world between establishing religion and using religion as a motivation for our action. The fact that the state is prohibited from establishing a religion does not mean that we can't allow the language of that motivation to have its legitimate place in the public square. Government should never screen out people of faith who believe that their understanding of God's Word serves as their motivation and guide for their public and private lives and decisions.

As is shown in the lives and words of the people we have discussed in this chapter, we would be a much different country, and not for the better, if that were true. And if your politics lean more to the left side of the spectrum, it is worth noting that it isn't just conservative Republicans who seek to bring religious language to the public square. President Lyndon Johnson was famous for quoting Isaiah 1:18, "Come now, let us reason together." President Obama also relied on biblical language to justify his positions. During a White House meeting I attended with other governors, Obama cited his concern for "the least of these" in replying to a question about why he wouldn't give states more control over their Medicaid programs.

If you need another reason to place a high value on people of faith in our community, consider the difference faith makes in volunteering, generous giving, and civic activism. In his book *American Grace*, Robert Putnam, Harvard professor of public policy, writes about the remarkable difference in the traits of good neighborliness between religious and nonreligious people. Basing his observations on the 2006 Faith Matters Survey, Putnam found a remarkable and consistent gap between religious and nonreligious people that held steady regardless of demographic or political ideology. After noting how much more people of faith contribute to their communities in time, dollars, and neighborliness, Putnam remarked that those differences were true regardless of the backgrounds and demographics of the people being compared. "Every significant generalization in this chapter remains accurate when we control simultaneously for gender, education, income, race, region, homeownership, length of residence, marital and parental status, ideology and age."[15]

Perhaps it isn't too surprising that church members would volunteer more for religious causes. After all, church membership provides a lot of opportunities to volunteer, from keeping the nursery and teaching Sunday school to serving meals at the church. What is surprising in the survey is that church members are more likely to volunteer for secular organizations in addition to their religious commitments. Putnam cites Giving and Volunteering surveys sponsored by the Independent Sector from 1988 to 2001, saying, "45 percent of weekly churchgoers report nonreligious volunteering (in addition to whatever religious volunteering they do), as compared to 26 percent of nonchurchgoers."[16]

The difference is just as notable when it comes to philanthropic giving. Americans are, relative to the rest of the world, generous givers. However, there are big differences between the giving of religious Americans and secular Americans. Putnam says, "Measuring charitable giving as a fraction of annual income, the average person in the most religious fifth of Americans is more than four times as generous as his or her counterpart in the least religious fifth, roughly 7 percent vs. roughly 1.5 percent."[17] And, as with volunteering, the results are not due to religious givers giving only to religious causes. "Regular churchgoers are more likely to give to secular causes than nonchurchgoers, and highly religious people give a larger fraction of their income to secular causes than do most secular people."[18] The net effect is that religious people are better givers to secular causes as well as religious causes.

In addition, frequent churchgoers are more likely to give

blood, help someone find a job, and even allow a stranger to cut in front of them. The last example being particularly helpful in these days of road rage! As Putnam says, "In particular, religiously observant Americans are more generous with time and treasure than demographically similar secular Americans. This is true for secular causes (especially help to the needy, the elderly, and young people) as well as for purely religious causes. It is true even for most random acts of kindness."[19]

And, when it comes to civic engagement, religious Americans are far more likely to be involved in community organizations, such as the Boy Scouts, United Way, or Red Cross. In addition, "Of the most religious Americans, 56 percent report that they vote in 'all or most local elections' compared to 46 percent of the most secular Americans."[20]

When men and women enter the arena with a truly faithful presence, the world is changed as a result of their vision. Doors have been opened, hospitals have been started, education has been provided, injustices have been addressed, and jobs have been created. Requiring a secular approach to our public discussions would remove a critical source of passion and motivation to make the world more just and merciful. Even those who think they would like a public square devoid of any religious presence would likely find themselves disappointed with the end result of a rigid secularism.

People of faith should take courage, instruction, and inspiration from the men and women who have come before us and have faithfully entered the public square. Our call to the arena may look like running for office or simply being a better neighbor and a more involved and informed citizen. Whatever the call, it is ours to answer with a passion for justice, a love of mercy, and a spirit of humility.

14

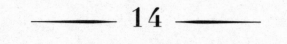

IT STARTS WITH US

I was standing on the tarmac at Memphis International Airport waiting on Air Force One to arrive. It is hard not to be excited and impressed when the gigantic light-blue-and-white Boeing VC-25, with UNITED STATES OF AMERICA painted on the side, slowly comes to a stop in front of you. This time I was standing with Memphis mayor A. C. Wharton. Prior to being elected mayor of Memphis, he had been the first African American mayor of Shelby County. Understandably, he was excited about welcoming Barack Obama, the first African American president of the United States, to his city.

Mayor Wharton became even more excited when President Obama descended the steps of Air Force One and invited us to ride with him in the presidential limousine. While the president worked his way down the rest of the receiving line, Secret Service agents approached the mayor and me to tell us where we should sit in the limousine. They told me to sit in the left front-facing seat next to the president.

I had strained my back a few days before, so I gingerly lowered myself into my seat by bracing against the center console between the president's seat and mine. As I did, my finger accidentally hit the president's seat warmer button and turned it on high. This was summertime in Memphis, where the heat and humidity beg for air conditioning, not seat warmers on high. As I sat back in my seat, I realized what I had done. Unfortunately, the president was settling into his seat at the exact same moment and felt the warmth of his seat. He gave me a questioning grin and said, "Well, that is an uncomfortable way to get started."

Unlike my accidental uncomfortable beginning in the presidential limousine, Jesus frequently begins in uncomfortable places on purpose. And he usually begins with us, the religious types. The older brother who had to be reminded that it was time to celebrate when his prodigal younger brother came back home. The church leaders who grumbled when Jesus announced that he was going to the house of a tax collector whom everyone except Jesus seemed to know was a horrible sinner. Jesus never allowed the religious crowd to focus on what other people were doing wrong.

So, as we look with discouragement at what feels like a deteriorating public square, our first questions have to be about ourselves—a very uncomfortable place to start.

When a woman was caught in the act of adultery, an angry mob brought her to Jesus. (It is more than interesting that it was only the woman who was brought before Jesus, since, in this case, she'd had to have a partner to be guilty.) The crowd was certain that this religious teacher would verify that her penalty for adultery should be death by stoning.

After all, there wasn't any doubt about her guilt, and the law was clear on this one. As they held the rocks in their hands and waited for Jesus' signal to go ahead, he turned the tables on them. In one of the most quoted lines of all time, Jesus said, "Let him who is without sin among you be the first to throw a stone at her" (John 8:7). When the crowd heard his reply, the Bible says, "they went away one by one, beginning with the older ones" (v. 9). To be clear, this is not an argument that adultery was just fine with Jesus. The story does end with him telling the woman to "go, and from now on sin no more" (v. 11). The call to repent, to change

190

her life, was about as clear as could be. But the primary message was for the religious types who were calling to stone the woman. The religious people wanted to make an example of her so they could use her for their own purposes. Jesus' response was to say to the religious leaders, "Let's talk about you first. I will talk to her later." There is a fine line between righteousness and self-righteousness. God loves the former and hates the latter.

Jesus turned the tables another time on the religious crowd, literally. He had just returned to Jerusalem and had made a triumphal entry, greeted by adoring crowds. As he entered the city, the crowd was shouting, "Blessed is he who comes in the name of the Lord! Hosanna in the highest!" (Matthew 21:9). As a recovering politician, I can tell you that when the crowd is with you, the last thing you want to do is go against the crowd. If there had been political polls in those days, Jesus' numbers would have been at their highest level. This was not the time to straighten out the crowd. Yet Jesus chose this time to go into the temple and flip over the tables of the people who were using religious ceremony for their own profit.

This story is a sobering reminder for any of us who are tempted to use God to accomplish our own objectives. The money changers and pigeon sellers had found a nice business with a religious purpose. But they were doing it for their own gain—and using the house of God no less. Jesus used strong language to rebuke them. "It is written, 'My house shall be called a house of prayer,' but you make it a den of robbers" (Matthew 21:13).

All of us in politics and everywhere else should be careful to make sure we are being used by God, not using God for our own ends. As with the crowd who brought the adulterous woman to Jesus, he had no patience for those who would use God to score their own points. More often than not, Jesus rebuked the religious, and his sights seemed to be particularly set on those who would use God to serve their own ends.

INEFFECTIVE SALT

This focus first on those who would be considered God's people was consistent with Jesus' message. Jesus told his followers that they were to be "the salt of the earth" (Matthew 5:13). Today, *Merriam-Webster* defines *salt of the earth* as "a very good and honest person or group of people."[1] Jesus had a much higher expectation than that for them. They were and are to be people who do for the world what salt did for meat in the days before refrigeration: keep it from spoiling. If the meat went bad, it was the salt's fault, not the meat's. The point for Christians then, and now, is that we are the ones who are supposed to be the preservatives in our communities and countries. If we feel as if things are going from bad to worse in our world, then maybe we should ask questions of ourselves first. If the culture around us in our spheres of influence is deteriorating, maybe it is because we have lost our saltiness. Jesus went on to say that if salt loses its saltiness, "it is no longer good for anything except to be thrown out and trampled under people's feet" (Matthew 5:13). Strong language again.

If Jesus' prescription for change was always to start with ourselves, and if we all desire for our public square to be a place that solves problems and brings life, then how should the followers of Jesus lead in the effort to do that?

We can start by knowing that we never have the right to be self-righteous or condescending or disdainful in public debate or anywhere else. We should be agents of civility because we know we have been saved only by the grace of a merciful God. We are not better people than others—far from it. We join G. K. Chesterton, who said, "What is wrong with the world? I am."[2]

For many of us, that is a hard truth to own. Understanding our own brokenness is key to understanding ourselves and, most importantly, why Jesus came to redeem us.

Imagine if that were the first thing people thought of when they thought of Christians in the public square. What if, when asked about Christians as a part of the public debate, their response was, "Finally, there are some voices in the debate who are more committed to making a difference than making their point"? Because we know we bring our own brokenness into the conversation, and we know our own selfishness and sinfulness means that we understand we might not have all the right answers, we are the people who are seeking to help find the best answer, not just our answer. What a difference that would make.

SEASONED

When I teach college students, I notice it is much easier for them to fix on the idea of institutional sinfulness rather than personal sinfulness. Both are real. Many of our institutions, beginning with our churches but including our corporations, governments, and other agencies, have earned a diminishing lack of respect from people of all generations. Injustice is built into many of our institutions, and it needs to be pointed out and addressed.

But when it comes to our personal sinfulness, that can be a little harder to own. It is a lot easier to say that the fault is somewhere out there. However, that is less than helpful if we are seeking to follow Jesus' lead and take a look at our own hearts first. It takes the recognition that, in the words of Aleksandr Solzhenitsyn, "the line separating good and evil passes not through states, nor between classes, nor between political parties either—but right through every human heart."[3]

For me, the older I get, the more I recognize my own shortcomings. Even in the course of writing this book, I have found myself incapable of following my own advice. I find myself getting angry when I read an editorial I disagree with or watch a news program that slants the truth away from my perspective. I find it hard to see the image of God in someone I disagree with. I think Chesterton is right about what is wrong with the world. It's me.

Whenever I had the opportunity to appoint judges, I looked for self-awareness, those who recognized their own fallibility. Because we interviewed everyone whose nominations were placed before us, I had multiple chances to consider the characteristics that were most important for such a critical position. Early on, one of the members of our legal team referred to a candidate as having been "seasoned by life." Over time, as we interviewed and selected more and more judges, the legal team and I came to value that trait more and more.

It didn't mean that we were looking only for older candidates. Some people can live a lifetime and not learn many lessons. It did mean that we placed a higher value on candidates who had endured the scrapes and bruises of life and had come to understand their own failings and shortcomings. We were trying to avoid selecting judges who would be subject to "black robe syndrome" and begin thinking they were somehow above the people who came before them. I believe the best judges are those men and women who can make decisions regarding other people with a commitment to justice while at the same time maintaining an awareness of the mercy we all need. They are judges who will be "peaceable, gentle, open to reason, full of mercy and good fruits, impartial and sincere" (James 3:17) as they fulfill their responsibility to provide justice.

Similarly, in business, I often found that employees who had owned their own business before coming to work with us had a different level of understanding. They knew things didn't always work out and that businesses don't always thrive or even survive. Because of that, their decisions reflected a different level of wisdom.

Maybe that is why the older ones were the first to drop their stones when Jesus gave his famous call for the one "who is without sin" to cast the first stone (John 8:7–9). They, too, had been seasoned by life.

I believe that is how those of us who call ourselves Christians, regardless of how old we are, can begin to change our level of political conversation. We can enter the public square with full knowledge of our own shortcomings and a commitment to being open to reason. If we begin there, we are free to seek the best answer and not just our answer. Committed to truth, but with gentleness, being full of mercy and open to reason. That would breathe fresh life into a world that is exhausted from two sides shouting at each other.

WHAT GOVERNMENT CANNOT DO

If we are going to have a faithful presence in the public arena, we also have to recognize the limits of what government can do—and see what people of faith are called to do to stand in that gap. Recently, Christians have landed on politics as the best way to enable the change we desire. I believe in the political process and agree with Martin Luther that we should send our best to serve in political roles.[4] And one of the main points that I have tried to make in this book is that we are all called to have a presence of some type as citizens in the arena.

But we also have to realize the limits of what government can do. After being elected to office, I quickly learned that government is a lot better at fixing potholes than we are at fixing hearts.

Our primary focus in the governor's office was public education, from kindergarten through college. I felt then, and still believe now, that education is a civil rights issue, and we have for too long accepted the idea that it was normal for some students in some areas to not have great education. I also firmly believe that education is an economic equity issue and that our income inequality issues will only grow starker if we don't become more serious about increasing the educational opportunities for all students.

I was, and still am, passionate about the policies we advocated to improve education. In office I strongly believed in raising our standards and expectations for what students should master every step of their educational journey. It is important that "all" really does mean "all" when it comes to saying that *all* children can learn. I think it is critical that we have a way to assess what students are learning so we can identify approaches that aren't working.

With all that being said, there are many things that cannot be addressed through education policy initiatives. If you spend any time at all inside a school, you realize that a lot of societal problems walk through the front door of that school every morning. Our teachers spend a lot of time on things that don't have anything to do with reading, writing, or arithmetic. Children whose parents are going through a divorce or are no longer at home walk through those doors every morning. Parents who have lost their jobs or are suffering from opiate addiction pull up in the line to drop their kids off every morning. It is a lot easier to come up with education policy initiatives than it is to solve issues of the heart.

I use education policy as an example to remind us of the limits of government. Regardless of who we elect to Congress, the White House, or the statehouse, these matters of the heart will not be solved by legislative action. Samuel Johnson got it right when he wrote, "How small, of all that human hearts endure, / That part which laws or kings can cause or cure!"[5] The good news is that those matters of the heart are things Christians are equipped to address as people who have Christ dwelling in us (Ephesians 3:17).

Bob Pierce was a founder of World Vision, a Christian humanitarian agency that works with people in poverty in more than one hundred countries across the globe. Pierce's prayer was, "Let my heart be broken with the things that break the heart of God."[6] Are the things that break our hearts the things that break God's heart? Our hearts tend to be broken by those things that don't work out the way we wanted them to work out. Our candidate did not get elected. The other side seems to be winning the public argument. The news media keeps getting the story wrong. But our hearts should be more preoccupied with the things God cares about. And that should be the launching point for our presence in the public square.

Right about now it would be fair for the reader to wonder why I am talking about the limits of government in a book that is about encouraging readers to be a faithful presence in the public square. In the passage from Jeremiah that we discussed earlier, God asked the Israelites who were captive in Babylon to navigate a difficult tension. They were supposed to live as holy people, exiled in a strange land, and yet still seek the welfare of Babylon and the people who lived there. That is the same tension he is asking us to navigate.

We engage in politics because we know how much government can impact the common good, while we still realize the limits of what government can do to change hearts. We understand that tension because we also live with the tension of being called to be people of love and truth in a world that wants us to pick one or the other, as well as justice and mercy, even when we can't always clearly see how to do both.

Our response to a world that seems to be slipping out of control has too frequently been to enter the public square out of anger and with our focus on winning. Because of that, we have added contempt and division into the arena rather than helping to heal it. But God always starts with us when he talks about change. Again, if the meat has gone bad, it is the fault of the salt, not the meat. Those of us who call ourselves Christians now have the privilege and the responsibility of being God's ambassadors to a world that is weary and desperate for good news. There really isn't a plan B when it comes to God's plan for how the earth gets its salt.

If Jesus always starts with us, and we are the ones responsible for bringing salt and light into a world that is divided and angry, we need to develop a political theology—a theology that is as clear, coherent, and biblical as our vision for our marriages, jobs, and churches.

That biblical-political theology sometimes might leave us at odds with people of our political tribe. In fact, if it doesn't sometimes leave us at odds with them, it probably is not truly biblical. So, however we choose to have a faithful presence, we must commit to seeking justice, loving mercy, and walking humbly, not solely to win on certain critical issues.

—EPILOGUE—

UNTIL CHRIST IS FORMED IN YOU

We were on a trip to Asia to recruit business to Tennessee. Our flight from Seoul, South Korea, to Hangzhou, China, landed a couple of hours late, which was a problem since our first appointment was to visit a manufacturing company that was considering moving part of its operations to Tennessee. As a governor, when you travel inside the United States, a state trooper from your host state meets your flight and escorts you to your destination. That does not happen when you are traveling internationally, so we scrambled to grab our bags out of the overhead bins to get off the plane and to our meeting as soon as possible.

As we were moving from our seats to the aisle, Crissy said, "What's going on out there?" I looked out the window and saw a band and a large group of soldiers lined up outside the plane. I said, "I don't know, but it doesn't matter. We need to hurry." We headed down the aisle toward the plane door with the worn-out look that you have when you are fourteen time zones away from home.

The plane's exit took us directly down the stairs and onto the tarmac. As we stepped out of the plane and began to descend the stairs, the band started playing, and all the soldiers came to attention with a salute. At the bottom of the steps, an official gave Crissy the largest bouquet of roses I have ever seen. She later told me that it was more roses than I had given her in our entire marriage.

There was a brief ceremony, and then we were whisked into a

limousine and off we went without ever going through customs. Crissy and I were looking at each other, trying our hardest to understand what was happening. I leaned over to our host who was in the car with us and asked, "Can you tell me what that was all about?" He replied, "Do you really want to know?" I assured him we did. "It's not about you. Hangzhou is hosting world leaders for the G20 Summit in a month, and we were practicing."

It's not about you. That is a good message for all of us in the public arena. Whether as an elected official or a committed activist, the ability to affect the public debate can be intoxicating. All of us want to have a life that counts, that makes a difference. But all of us need to remember that the story is not about us. As Rick Warren said in *The Purpose Driven Life,* "It's not about you. The purpose of your life is far greater than your own personal fulfillment, your peace of mind, or even your happiness. It's far greater than your family, your career, or even your wildest dreams and ambitions."[1]

I would add that it is greater than our political success or the acceptance of our ideas. Maybe a fellow Jesuit eulogizing Saint Ignatius Loyola said it best: "The aim of life is not to gain a place in the sun, nor to achieve fame or success, but to lose ourselves in the glory of God." Our call is to be faithful, not successful. Our call is to be used by God, not to use God for our own desires. Like every other way in which we seek to be faithful, serving in the public arena can be a chance for us to grow into the people we were created to be. Paul told the Galatians he was "in the anguish of childbirth until Christ is formed in you" (Galatians 4:19). "Until Christ is formed in you" is what every Christian believer should be seeking.

Personally, nothing has affected my spiritual growth as much as campaigning and serving in public office. The heightened visibility and hard consequences of serving have frequently reminded me of my own weakness.

God used public office to change me. Some of that was due to the reality of knowing the job was bigger than me—that I couldn't make all the right decisions, solve all the problems, and keep everyone happy. Somewhere along the way I realized I really only had an audience of One and I needed to be faithful to the One. It was also the result of the humbling feeling that comes from knowing the decisions we were making would impact a lot of people and hoping our decisions would serve those people well. Through it all, God continually reminded me of his faithfulness to me over time.

I have kept a prayer journal for many years. When I flip back through those journals, I am reminded of the things that were on my heart and mind during those days. Months and years after the fact, I can look back and see that those things that caused me such anxiety at the time—those are the things God used to show me that "the steadfast love of the LORD never ceases; his mercies never come to an end; they are new every morning; great is your faithfulness" (Lamentations 3:22–23). When I was writing this book, I looked at those journals several times to try and remember what I was thinking during a campaign or some critical event. I was struck by the fact that God shaped me more by the things that didn't work out the way we wanted than when we won on an issue we cared about.

The idea that God can use our engagement in the public square to make us more like him ultimately led me to write about what a faithful presence in that square can look like. Believe me, I struggled for a long time with whether I should write this book. I have read enough books to know that very few books really change anyone's thoughts or actions. I also know that I was definitely not the perfect mayor or governor. I made a lot of mistakes. Not just in policy or execution of our plans but also in the way I personally handled situations. One of the downsides to being in public office is that your warts and blemishes are there for everyone to see. So it feels a bit hypocritical to write a book prescribing how we can address the seeming hopelessness of our political culture when I know there were so many things I could have done better or handled differently.

In the end, I decided to write the book because I truly believe that times like this require people who understand justice *and* mercy, people who know truth *and* love, and people who know that we need to engage for the common good *and* not put all our hopes in political outcomes. It would be easy to give up and say I am too angry at the other side or too exhausted with the process to keep going. But we are all called to seek the peace of the places where God has called us.

As a divided and angry America faces off against itself, we have the privilege of being a part of a bigger story that God is writing. Every now and then, like with my story with Cyntoia, we get the chance to see how our part of the story intersects with others in the tapestry that God is weaving.

My last day in office was spent the way I imagine most governors spend their last days. Even though I obviously knew that day was coming, and I had the best of intentions to be packed up early, we spent that Friday taking care of details and packing boxes. Crissy came over to join me that afternoon, and we walked around the capitol thanking people one last time for all their great work. Finally, we finished up and walked out the door and down those steps one last time as governor and first lady. I wasn't sad. We'd had our turn, and it was now time for Governor Lee and his team to take over. I was exceedingly grateful for the opportunity to be the governor of a state I love.

As our SUV pulled out and headed down the capitol driveway, I saw both sides of the road lined with folks from our staff team. They were holding campaign signs from eight years earlier. Many of them had brought their children with them, few of whom had been born when we came to Nashville. Some of them were team members who had left for other opportunities but had come back for this going-away surprise. All of them were people Crissy and I had come to truly appreciate for the selfless way they served. We jumped out of the car to hug everyone and thank them again one last time. When it came time to say something, a lump formed in my throat, and I had a hard time getting any words out. When I could finally speak, the first thing that came to mind was David's words: "Who am I, O Lord GOD, and what is my house, that you have brought me thus far?" (2 Samuel 7:18).

Amazingly, God has called all of us to be a part of what he is doing. Frankly, that doesn't always make sense to me. Why use broken, unfaithful people like us? Because he created us in his image. Then he sent his own Son to show us what justice and mercy look like and to model truth and love at the same time. What he asks of us is that we enter those places where he has called us with humility, knowing that we don't have all the answers and that sometimes we will get it wrong. As G. K. Chesterton wrote, "a man was meant to be doubtful about himself, but undoubting about the truth."[2]

By seeking to have a faithful presence in the public arena, we should seek the peace of these places where we have been called—and in doing that, help this world to look a little more like the world that is to come.

ACKNOWLEDGMENTS

I have a new respect for anyone who has written a book. This is way harder than it looks. And like everything else that I have ever done, it required the help of a lot of people. There is no way to properly acknowledge all the people who helped make this book better.

Similarly, it is impossible to thank all the people who were on our teams at the city of Knoxville and the state of Tennessee. And I would never even have had the chance to serve without all those who helped me get elected. Very few of our best ideas were my ideas, and even less of the implementation. I have repeatedly been blessed with great team members. I would love to write about so many of them, but that would be almost another book. If you are one of those team members, please know that I am always available to help you if I can ever repay you for everything you did for me.

I am not sure how many conversations I have had on this book or how many people have helped me think through the ideas that are presented. There are so many people who encouraged me and made this book better with their input. My biggest fear is the reality that I will neglect to mention someone who deserves credit. Let me apologize in advance, and please blame my head and not my heart

The team at Nelson Books has been patient and long suffering with this rookie writer. I know they hung up the phone or put down their keypad after many exchanges with me wondering if I had any clue what I was doing. Webb Younce, Jessica Wong, Sujin Hong, Sara Broun, Stephanie Tresner, Phoebe Wetherbee, Kristina Juodenas, Chenal Patton, Timothy Paulson, and Mark Schoenwald all deserve medals for their patience, trust, and guidance in helping me through this process. John Sloan taught me about how a book should flow and what helps a reader to keep reading. Trust me, if that didn't happen in this book, it is due to the pupil and not the teacher. And my longtime friend Robert Wolgemuth has been a constant source of wisdom as my agent. Despite battling cancer through much of this process, he has always been available and encouraging. I am grateful for all the professionals who have helped with this book. I also want to thank Frances Slatery, who was very helpful with some of the early research.

My Nashville Monday Morning Group are friends for the ages who showed up to pray every Monday morning at the Governor's Residence. Though there is a chance they were just coming for the free breakfast, I know that Greg Adams, Tom Douglas, Scott Sauls, Herbert Slatery, Troy Tomlinson, and Gif Thornton added depth, wisdom, and a lot of laughter to my life. Longtime friends Chip and Desiree Denton, Steve and Cathy Chesney, Rick and Jill Woolworth, David and Lee Bowen, Don and Robbin Flow, Meg and Terry Troutman, Bob and Lisa Nesbitt, and Rodney and Dell Lawler either reviewed the manuscript or were a part of conversations that helped shape my thinking.

Real authors like Donald Miller, Russell Moore, Richard Stearns, and Jon Meacham were kind enough to read the book and give helpful feedback. Pastors and friends John Wood and Doug Banister provided theological insight and encouragement. James Davidson Hunter not only let me steal his phrase *faithful presence* for my title, but he also provided perspective and wisdom that I could never have on my own.

During much of the time that I was writing this book, I was also serving as board chair of Young Life. I cannot count the number of conversations I have had with the amazing men and women on Young Life staff around the world who added to my thoughts about what a faithful presence might look like. Friends like Raja Jubran, David Reynolds, Bo Campbell, and so many others have consistently put helping me above their own needs. For almost twenty years, Janet McGaha has been my assistant. She has solved problems, smoothed ruffled feelings, picked up the balls that I dropped, and always made whatever office we were in a more fun place to be for everyone.

I had the opportunity to serve with so many great public servants during my time in office. I particularly want to thank Bob Corker and Lamar Alexander who served as Tennessee's US senators during my time in office. Both of them made my time as governor easier and made Tennessee a better state. In addition, I had the blessing of handing the governor's office to a friend and brother when Bill Lee succeeded me. It is a lot easier to leave when you have confidence in the next person.

Finally, I always say that I hit the lottery when it comes to having a great family. Jimmy and Dee Haslam and Ann and Steve Bailey have knocked on doors, asked their friends to donate to campaigns, encouraged me, and suffered the slings and arrows that come with having a relative in office. Our dad, Jim Haslam, taught us all that it matters who we elect and that we all need to be involved in the political process. Beyond that, he has modeled a life of unselfishness and giving. We need more people like him. Natalie Haslam has loved my father so well and has loved me like her own. Her quiet wisdom and strength make it easy to love her back.

It is a wonderful thing when you have children and their spouses whom you can consider friends and sources of wisdom. I have learned so much from Will, Hannah, Annie, David, Leigh, and Matt, and I am proud of the ways that they are walking through life in their own callings. Times with them and our ten grandchildren grow my heart and expand my vision for what it means to follow Jesus.

I met Crissy on my first day of college, though it took me a little while to convince her to date me. Although she "had me at hello," my love and respect and appreciation only grows and grows after forty years together. One of the best surprises about being governor was that it was a job we got to do together. From campaigning all across the state to working to provide better educational outcomes for students, it was always better because Crissy was by my side. I am forever grateful for her.

NOTES

CHAPTER 1: DIVIDED AND ANGRY

1. Encyclopedia Britannica Online, "United States Presidential Election Results," updated February 3, 2017, https://www .brittanica.com/topic/United-States-Presidential-Election -Results-1788863.

2. John Whitesides, "From Disputes to a Breakup: Wounds Still Raw After U.S. Election," Reuters, February 7, 2017, https:// www.reuters.com/article/us-usa-trump-relationships-insight /from-disputes-to-a-breakup-wounds-still-raw-after-u-s-election -idUSKBN15M13L.

3. Ralph McGill, "Not a Very Wholesome Display," *Congressional Record*, August 28, 1967.

4. Robert W. Merry, *A Country of Vast Designs: James K. Polk, the Mexican War, and the Conquest of the American Continent* (New York: Simon & Schuster, 2009), 112.

5. Janet Adamy, "U.S. Marriage Rate Plunges to Lowest Level on Record," *Wall Street Journal*, April 29, 2020, https://www.wsj .com/articles/u-s-marriage-rate-plunges-to-lowest-level-on -record-11588132860.

6. Janet Adamy, "U.S. Birthrates Fall to Record Low," *Wall Street Journal*, May 20, 2020, https://www.wsj.com/articles/u-s -birthrates-fall-to-record-low-11589947260.

7. Elizabeth Wildsmith, Jennifer Manlove, and Elizabeth Cook,

"Dramatic Increase in the Proportion of Births Outside of Marriage in the United States from 1990 to 2016," ChildTrends, August 8, 2018, https://www.childtrends.org/publications /dramatic-increase-in-percentage-of-births-outside-marriage -among-whites-hispanics-and-women-with-higher-education -levels.

8. Mark Galli, "Trump Should Be Removed from Office," *Christianity Today*, December 19, 2019, https://www .christianitytoday.com/ct/2019/december-web-only/trump -should-be-removed-from-office.html.

9. U.S. National Archives and Records Administration, "President Abraham Lincoln's Second Inaugural Address (1865)," accessed December 3, 2020, https://www.ourdocuments.gov/doc .php?flash-false&doc=38#.

10. Timothy Keller and John Inazu, *Uncommon Ground: Living Faithfully in a World of Difference* (Nashville: Nelson Books, 2020), xviii.

11. David French, "Coronavirus, Conspiracy Theories, and the Ninth Commandment," *The Dispatch* (blog), July 19, 2020, https:// frenchpress.thedispatch.com/p/coronavirus-conspiracy -theories-and.

CHAPTER 2: WHAT IS HAPPENING NOW?
1. Arthur Brooks, *Love Your Enemies: How Decent People Can Save America from the Culture of Contempt* (New York: Broadside Books, 2019).

2. Eliza Collins, "Les Moonves: Trump's Run Is 'Damn Good for CBS,'" Politico, February 29, 2016, https://www.politico.com /blogs/on-media/2016/02/les-moonves-trump-cbs-220001.

3. Jeremy Hsu, "People Choose News That Fits Their Views," Live Science, June 7, 2009, https://www.livescience.com/3640 -people-choose-news-fits-views.html.

4. Boston College, "Study Finds Intractable Conflicts Stem from Misunderstanding of Motivation," ScienceDaily, November 4, 2014, https://www.sciencedaily.com/releases/2014/11 /141104083946.htm.

5. Pew Research Center, *Partisanship and Political Animosity in*

2016, June 22, 2016, https://www.pewresearch.org/politics
/2016/06/22/1-feelings-about-partisans-and-the-parties/.

6. David Wasserman, "To Beat Trump, Democrats May Need
to Break Out of the 'Whole Foods' Bubble," *New York Times*,
February 27, 2020, https://www.nytimes.com/interactive
/2020/02/27/upshot/democrats-may-need-to-break-out-of
-the-whole-foods-bubble.html; and Michael Hendrix, "Why
2016 Came Down to Whole Foods vs. Cracker Barrel," Medium,
November, 10, 2016, https://medium.com/@michael_hendrix
/why-2016-came-down-to-whole-foods-vs-cracker-barrel
-4361cb9b1e5f.

CHAPTER 3: CONFUSED, INEFFECTIVE, AND EXHAUSTED

1. Pew Research Center, *In U.S., Decline of Christianity
Continues at Rapid Pace*, October 17, 2019, https://www
.pewforum.org/2019/10/17/in-u-s-decline-of-christianity
-continues-at-rapid-pace/.

2. Friedrich Nietzsche, *Beyond Good and Evil: Prelude to a
Philosophy of the Future*, trans. Helen Zimmern (New York:
Macmillan, 1907), 97.

3. Isaiah Berlin, "The Originality of Machiavelli," in *The Proper
Study of Mankind: An Anthology of Essays* (1949; repr., London:
Random House, 1998), 289.

4. C. S. Lewis, "Meditation on the Third Commandment," in *God
in the Dock*, ed. Walter Hooper (Grand Rapids, MI: William B.
Eerdmans, 1970), 196–99.

5. Nathan Hatch, "The Political Captivity of the Faithful,"
Comment, February 13, 2020, https://www.cardus.ca/comment
/article/the-political-captivity-of-the-faithful/.

6. Anne Case and Angus Deaton, *Deaths of Despair and the Future of
Capitalism* (Princeton, NJ: Princeton University Press, 2020).

7. Centers for Disease Control and Prevention, "U.S. Drug
Overdose Deaths Continue to Rise; Increase Fueled by Synthetic
Opioids," press release, March 29, 2018, https://www.cdc.gov
/media/releases/2018/p0329-drug-overdose-deaths.html, and
"Suicide Rates Rising Across the U.S.," press release, June 7,
2018, https://www.cdc.gov/media/releases/2018/p0607-suicide

-prevention.html; Alina Tugend, "Colleges Get Proactive in Addressing Depression on Campus," *New York Times*, June 7, 2017, https://www.nytimes.com/2017/06/07/education/colleges -get-proactive-in-addressing-depression-on-campus.html; and Emma Seppala and Peter Sims, "The Average American Has Only One Close Friend—Here's How We Got to This Point," *Business Insider*, July 16, 2017, https://www.businessinsider .com/emma-seppala-the-average-american-has-only-one-close -friend-2017-7.

CHAPTER 4: WHY SHOULD WE CARE ABOUT THE
PUBLIC GOOD?

1. Martin Luther, "Treatise on Good Works," in *Works of Martin Luther*, vol. 1, trans. C. M. Jacobs (1519; repr., Philadelphia: A. J. Holman, 1915).
2. Adams to the officers of the First Brigade of the Third Division of the Militia of Massachusetts, October 11, 1798, in *The Works of John Adams*, vol. 9 (Boston: Little, Brown, 1854), 229.
3. Timothy Keller, "The Closing of the Modern Mind," Veritas Forum, New York University, March 1, 2017, http://www.veritas .org/closing-modern-mind-tim-keller-jonathan-haidt-nyu -full-version.

CHAPTER 5: IF THE MEEK WILL INHERIT THE EARTH,
WHO WILL RUN FOR OFFICE?

1. C. S. Lewis, *Mere Christianity* (New York: Simon & Schuster, 1996), 109, 111.
2. Jack Miller, quoted in Tullian Tchividjian, *Surprised by Grace: God's Relentless Pursuit of Rebels* (Wheaton, IL: Crossway, 2010), 44.
3. Morning Prayer, in *Book of Common Prayer*, http://justus .anglican.org/~ss/commonworship/word/morningbcp.html.
4. D. Martyn Lloyd-Jones, *Studies in the Sermon on the Mount* (Grand Rapids, MI: William B. Eerdmans, 1971), 68.
5. David Brooks, *The Road to Character* (New York: Random House, 2015), 3.
6. Brooks, *Road to Character*, 3.

7. Brooks, *Road to Character*, 4.

8. Dwight D. Eisenhower, quoted in Scott Simon, "The Speech Eisenhower Never Gave on the Normandy Invasion," *Weekend Edition Saturday*, NPR, June 8, 2013, https://www.npr.org /2013/06/08/189535104/the-speech-eisenhower-never-gave -on-the-normandy-invasion.

CHAPTER 6: IS IT HARD TO BE A CHRISTIAN IN POLITICS?

1. J. R. R. Tolkien, *The Lord of the Rings* (1955; repr., New York: Houghton Mifflin Harcourt, 2005). The quote is from the movie.

CHAPTER 7: DOES MEEKNESS HAVE A CHANCE?

1. Jim Collins, *Good to Great: Why Some Companies Make the Leap . . . and Others Don't* (New York: HarperBusiness, 2001), 5–6.

2. Collins, *Good to Great*, 12–13.

3. Robert P. Abelson and James C. Miller, "Negative Persuasion via Personal Insult," *Journal of Experimental Social Psychology* 3, no. 4 (October 1967): 3, 321–33.

4. Lincoln to General Ulysses S. Grant, July 13, 1863, in Abraham Lincoln Online, http://www.abrahamlincolnonline.org/lincoln /speeches/grant.htm.

5. Abraham Lincoln, "Address to the 166th Ohio Regiment," August 22, 1864, https://www.nps.gov/liho/learn/historyculture /thankstotroops.htm.

6. Arthur C. Brooks, *Love Your Enemies: How Decent People Can Save America from the Culture of Contempt* (New York: Broadside Books, 2019), 53.

7. *Strong's Concordance*, s.v. "tapeinos," accessed December 2, 2020, https://biblehub.com/greek/5011.htm.

CHAPTER 8: CREATED IN THE IMAGE OF WHOM?

1. C. S. Lewis, *The Weight of Glory* (San Francisco: HarperOne, 2001), 45–46.

2. Lewis, *Weight of Glory*, 45–46.

3. Peggy Noonan, "What Comes After the Coronavirus Storm?"

Wall Street Journal, April 23, 2020, https://www.wsj.com/articles
/what-comes-after-the-coronavirus-storm-11587684752.

4. Peter Frankopan, *The Silk Roads: A New History of the World*
(New York: Vintage Books, 2017), 360–63.

5. Lewis, *Weight of Glory*, 45–46.

6. Martin Luther King Jr., "The American Dream" (sermon
delivered at Ebenezer Baptist Church, Atlanta, GA, July 4,
1965), The Martin Luther King Jr. Research and Education
Institute at Stanford University, https://kinginstitute.stanford
.edu/king-papers/publications/knock-midnight-inspiration-great
-sermons-reverend-martin-luther-king-jr-4.

Chapter 9: What About the Separation of Church and State?

1. Bill Haslam, veto letter, April 14, 2016, http://content-static
.tennessean.com/PDFs/HaslamVetoLetter.pdf.

2. Originally written as "citty upon a hill." John M. Barry, *Roger
Williams and the Creation of the American Soul: Church, State, and
the Birth of Liberty* (New York: Penguin, 2012), 2–4.

3. Barry, *Roger Williams and the Creation of the American Soul*, 2–4.

4. Ben Sasse, *Them: Why We Hate Each Other—and How to Heal*
(New York: St. Martin's Publishing Group, 2018), 149.

5. Sasse, *Them*, 149–50.

6. Adams to the officers of the First Brigade of the Third Division
of the Militia of Massachusetts, October 11, 1798, in *The Works
of John Adams*, vol. 9 (Boston: Little, Brown, 1854), 229.

7. Peter Wehner, *The Death of Politics: How to Heal Our Frayed
Republic After Trump* (San Francisco: HarperOne, 2019), 63.

8. Masterpiece Cakeshop v. Colorado Civil Rights Commission,
584 US (2018), https://www.supremecourt.gov/opinions/17pdf
/16-111_j4el.pdf.

9. Masterpiece Cakeshop v. Colorado Civil Rights Commission, 3.

10. "Nondiscrimination FAQ," Vanderbilt University, https://www.
vanderbilt.edu/about/nondiscrimination/faq.php.

11. Tamarie Macon, "The Closing of the Modern Mind," Veritas
Forum, New York University, March 1, 2017, http://www.veritas

.org/closing-modern-mind-tim-keller-jonathan-haidt-nyu-full-version/.

12. John D. Inazu, *Confident Pluralism: Surviving and Thriving Through Deep Difference* (Chicago: University of Chicago Press, 2018), 187–88.

13. Inazu, *Confident Pluralism*, 187–88.

14. Associated Press, "Tennessee Lawmakers Confuse Mop Sink in State Capitol for Muslim Foot-Washing Sink," *Chattanooga Times Free Press*, March 26, 2013, https://www.timesfreepress.com /news/local/story/2013/mar/26/tennessee-lawmakers-confuse -mop-sink-state-capitol/103410/.

Chapter 12: What Does a Faithful Presence Look Like?

1. James Davison Hunter, *To Change the World* (Oxford: Oxford University Press, 2010), 277.

2. This quote from *Knoxville Journal and Tribune*, December 1900, is engraved on the sidewalk of Market Square.

3. C. S. Lewis, *Mere Christianity* (New York: Simon & Schuster, 1996).

Chapter 13: A Few Examples and Why It Matters

1. Salem Chapel, January 5, 2015, http://salemchapelbmechurch.ca /news--disclaimer.html.

2. Harriet Tubman, as told to biographer Sarah H. Bradford, quoted in William J. Bennett and John T. E. Cribb, *The American Patriot's Almanac* (Nashville: Thomas Nelson, 2008), 154.

3. Quoted in David S. Shields, *Oracles of Empire* (Chicago: University of Chicago Press, 1990), 77.

4. "William Wilberforce: Antislavery Politician," Christian History, *Christianity Today*, accessed December 2, 2020, https://www .christianitytoday.com/history/people/activists/william -wilberforce.html.

5. "William Wilberforce," Christian History, *Christianity Today*.

6. "William Wilberforce," Christian History, *Christianity Today*.

7. Martin Luther King Jr., "Letter from a Birmingham Jail," April 16, 1963, http://okra.stanford.edu/transcription /document_images/undecided/630416–019.pdf.

8. John Lewis, "John Lewis Extended Interview," *Religion & Ethics Newsweekly*, PBS, January 16, 2004, https://www.pbs.org/wnet/religionandethics/2004/01/16/january-16–2004-john-lewis-extended-interview/2897/.

9. See George W. Bush, *Decision Points* (New York: Crown Publishers, 2010); and Michael J. Gerson, *Heroic Conservatism: Why Republicans Need to Embrace America's Ideals (And Why They Deserve to Fail If They Don't)* (San Francisco: HarperOne, 2008).

10. Nicholas Kristof, "He's Jesus Christ," *New York Times*, June 27, 2015, https://www.nytimes.com/2015/06/28/opinion/sunday/nicholas-kristof-hes-jesus-christ.html.

11. Kristof, "He's Jesus Christ."

12. John Rawls, "The Idea of Public Reason Revisited," *University of Chicago Law Review* 64, no. 3 (Summer 1997): 799.

13. George Will, "A Conversation with George F. Will," interview by Russell Moore, *Signposts*, December 4, 2019, https://www.russellmoore.com/2019/12/04/a-conversation-with-george-f-will/.

14. Stephen L. Carter, "Liberalism's Religion Problem," *First Things* (March 2002), https://www.firstthings.com/article/2002/03/liberalisms-religion-problem.

15. Robert D. Putnam and David E. Campbell, *American Grace: How Religion Divides and Unites Us* (New York: Simon & Schuster, 2010), 452.

16. Putnam and Campbell, *American Grace*, 445–46.

17. Putnam and Campbell, *American Grace*, 448.

18. Putnam and Campbell, *American Grace*, 448.

19. Putnam and Campbell, *American Grace*, 453.

20. Putnam and Campbell, *American Grace*, 455.

CHAPTER 14: IT STARTS WITH US

1. *Merriam-Webster*, s.v. "the salt of the earth," accessed December 2, 2020, https://www.merriam-webster.com/dictionary/the%20salt%20of%20the%20earth.

2. G. K. Chesterton, *What's Wrong with the World* (1910; repr., San Francisco: Ignatius Press, 1994).

3. Aleksandr Solzehnitsyn, quoted in Daniel J. Mahoney, *Aleksandr Solzhenitsyn: The Ascent from Ideology* (Oxford: Rowman & Littlefield, 2001), 50.
4. Martin Luther, "Treatise on Good Works," in *Works of Martin Luther*, vol. 1, trans. C. M. Jacobs (1519; repr., Philadelphia: A. J. Holman, 1915).
5. Samuel Johnson wrote the last few lines of the poem by Oliver Goldsmith, "The Traveller," December 19, 1764. Dinah Birch and Katy Hooper, eds., *The Concise Oxford Companion to English Literature*, 4th ed. (Oxford: Oxford University Press, 2012), 725.
6. Richard Stearns, *The Hole in Our Gospel: What Does God Expect of Us? The Answer That Changed My Life and Might Just Change the World* (Nashville: Thomas Nelson, 2009).

EPILOGUE: UNTIL CHRIST IS FORMED IN YOU

1. Rick Warren, *The Purpose Driven Life: What on Earth Am I Here For?* (Grand Rapids, MI: Zondervan, 2002), 17.
2. G. K. Chesterton, *Orthodoxy* (New York: 1908), 33, accessed December 2, 2020, https://www.fulltextarchive.com/pdfs /Orthodoxy-by-G-K-Chesterton.pdf.

ABOUT THE AUTHOR

Bill Haslam is the former two-term mayor of Knoxville, Tennessee, and former two-term governor of Tennessee. He was reelected in 2014 with the largest victory margin of any gubernatorial election in Tennessee history. During his tenure, Tennessee became the fastest-improving state in the country in K–12 education and the first state to provide free community college or technical school for all its citizens, in addition to adding 475,000 net new jobs. Haslam serves on the boards of Teach for America, the Wilson Center, and Young Life. He and his wife of over forty years, Crissy, have three children and ten grandchildren.